Accolades for *AUTHentic*

"A remarkable contribution to the fields of positive psychology, coaching and leadership. Applying the principles in this book will help you discover and leverage your strengths, improve your relationships and fulfill your potential—and help others do the same!"

—**Stephen M.R. Covey**, #1 bestselling author,
The Speed of Trust and *Smart Trust*

"Finally, an experienced voice in the world of leadership and personal coaching has built a model of personal growth that fully leverages the powerful set of tools we all possess—namely, our strengths of character. While other books on coaching make reference to the importance of building upon and building up personal strengths, this book is the first to make this strategy explicit and to unpack it practically for coaches. For a practical guide to helping your clients use their strengths of character to determine and pursue meaningful personal goals, read this book!"

—**Dr. Neal H. Mayerson**, Founder and Chairman,
VIA Institute on Character, Psychologist, and President,
The Mayerson Foundation

"By synthesizing evidence-based research and real-life stories, *Authentic Strengths* provides a brilliantly accessible toolbox for leading a happier, more successful life. This is an important book for you—if you are interested in making the most of your gifts and talents!"

—**Dr. Tal Ben-Shahar**, #1 bestselling author,
Happier and *Choose the Life You Want*;
taught Harvard's most popular course on Positive Psychology

"Grounded in the science of positive psychology, this book provides insights into human performance, leadership and well-being, and teaches practical ways to apply them in everyday life. A must-read for anyone interested in fulfilling their own potential or in coaching others to do so!"

—**Stephan Mardyks & David Covey,**
Co-CEOs and Co-Founders, SMCOV

"As a health and wellness expert, I find Fatima Doman's book *Authentic Strengths* to be an indispensable coaching guide for anyone wanting to increase their own well-being or the well-being of others. Doman brilliantly illustrates practical and proven strategies that empower people to recharge all four aspects of their being—mind, body, heart and spirit. This book is a must-read if you want to leverage your strengths to create a more vibrant and fulfilling life!"

—**Dr. Mark Hyman**, #1 bestselling author,
The Blood Sugar Solution, The UltraMind Solution, and *The 10-Day Detox Diet,*
Chairman, global Institute for Functional Medicine

"Dr. Mayerson's preface clearly lays out the value of this book, predicting it will soon be 'at the vanguard of establishing coaching excellence'—I could not agree more! As the founder and Faculty Director of Columbia University's Coaching Certification Program, and as an executive coach and consultant with more than thirty years of experience, I found Ms. Doman's ability to integrate theory, research and practice impressive, relevant and an important contribution to the emerging field of executive and organizational coaching. It is my hope that each reader gains the insights I've gained from this book. I will add it to the set of core resources that guide my professional coaching practice—congratulations, Fatima, on a job well done! Two thumbs up!"

—**Dr. Terrence E. Maltbia**, Founder and Faculty Director,
Columbia University Coaching Certification Program

"At long last! The first book to explicitly place character strengths—not talents or skills, but those best qualities most essential to who we are as human beings—at the forefront and core of the coaching process. If you're a coach dedicated to taking a substantive yet uplifting approach to helping your clients, this is the book to help inform, guide, and support you. Apply the concepts, questions, and exercises in this book and watch not only your clients flourish, but also yourself as well!"

—**Dr. Ryan M. Niemiec**, psychologist and bestselling author, *Mindfulness and Character Strengths: A Practical Guide to Flourishing*, Education Director, global, nonprofit VIA Institute on Character

"This book will help you reach your goals in a deceptively simple but transformative way—by learning to become an inner ally rather than being your own worst enemy."

—**Dr. Kristin Neff**, bestselling author, *Self Compassion*, Associate Professor, Human Development and Culture, University of Texas at Austin

"To win at 'the game of work' it is necessary to understand the strengths of all the team members and then to coach to those strengths to maximize effectiveness. This book gives any leader those essential elements and is well worth the time it will take to read and absorb its illuminating message. Thanks for this special contribution!"

—**Charles Coonradt**, bestselling author, *The Game of Work*, founder of GAME of WORK, Inc., "Grandfather of Gamification" according to Forbes

"If we business leaders had used this book in the past year, we would have doubtless reaped the benefits of a more engaged and energized workforce. I'm confident those benefits would have shown up on our bottom line. With this book, leaders can learn to recognize and unleash the collective strengths on their teams—and in the process build their credibility, career, and company!"

—**Kevin Cope**, CEO of Acumen Learning, #1 bestselling author, *Seeing the Big Picture: Business Acumen to Build Your Credibility, Career, and Company*

"This book focuses on character strengths and how using those strengths energizes people. While many books focus only on the effects of using one's strengths, this book focuses on the internal process and the approach of creating a positive state of mind and elevating human performance. We would like to show our appreciation for this book and the theory it is based on, which describes how strengths connect to well-being and flourishing. We believe this book will be a powerful guide for those who wish to use their character strengths to effectively lead others and to live a fulfilling life."

—**Business Consultants Inc.,** Japan, China and Korea

"I've worked with several NY Times bestselling authors and the level of integrity Fatima Doman has for her content and the passion with which she shares it is contagious and incredibly helpful to the reader. If you want to improve your life and the lives of others, connecting with this content is an indispensable part of your journey to transformational change."

—**Jacques Bazinet,** Vice President of Corporate Development at InsideOut Development, former Director in the Office of Stephen R. Covey

"Fatima Doman has a gift for helping people shift their perspective and leverage their strengths. The questions she asks here provoke a transformation as people come to learn and appreciate their own strengths and connect with their larger purpose. Bottom line: This is a holistic way of coaching and empowering people not just for business, but for life."

—**S. Max Brown**, VP of Leadership & Culture Pluralsight, author, *Leadership Vertigo*

"This is not simply a book—it is a powerful catalyst for positive and lasting change. An extraordinarily gifted coach and leader, Fatima Doman translates Positive Psychology theory into practical steps that can be applied to everyday life. This book is a must-read for every coach, leader, teacher, parent and anyone who wishes to truly maximize the power zone of their strengths!"

—**Jane Wundersitz** CEO and founder, WunderTraining Australia

"In India a Guru is a Coach. This book has taken the first step in showing the modern man the direction, in a simple yet scientific manner, toward SELF coaching and unlocks our hidden potential with the help of the Coach seated within. It is clearly mentioned in the Gita, and most wisdom literature, that every individual is born with unique STRENGTHS. This book explains how to tune into those strengths and create a life that is fulfilling and effective. Take the first step to self-transformation and glow from within. A must-read…Fatima Doman has written a book that will be a lighthouse to many. Life is about UNFOLDING the SELF."

—**Sunil Tapse**, Founder and CEO,
GR8SYNERGY, INDIA; Consultant for BP and Shell

"This groundbreaking book is an important contribution to the rapidly exploding field of positive psychology. Rooted in the 'science of happiness' and based upon the study of character strengths, *Authentic Strengths* lays out a road map for well-being that is both practical and easy to implement. It's an essential read for all of us striving to live a meaningful life and for coaches looking for a guidebook that will help them co-create plans for well-being with clients."

—**Dr. Sandra Scheinbaum**, Founder and CEO,
Functional Medicine Coaching Academy, Inc.,
author, *Stop Panic Attacks in 10 Easy Steps*

"Doman convincingly makes a case for recognizing and appreciating the strengths in those with whom you work. She demonstrates that leveraging those strengths is the currency of success in any relationship—personal or professional. This book is packed with time-honored wisdom that shows elevating strengths to be an indispensable leadership tool in the new global economy. A must-read for anyone seeking to unleash potential in themselves and the people around them!"

—**Brad McLaws**, Managing Partner of SagePoint Group,
Adjunct Professor at Marriott School of Management,
author, *Top Strategic Models*

"Football coaches understand that if they don't have a great playbook and the tools to transform that book into action, their team will not be successful on the field. Success coach Fatima Doman understands these same principles and has developed a playbook that will help you and your team (work, family, society, school, friends) succeed. My friend Fatima has pulled together an impressive array of research and coaching experiences, and she has distilled the information into a playbook that is easy to both follow and apply. Coaches of all varieties would do well to make this playbook an integral part of their 'game' preparation!"

—**Ryan E. Tibbitts**, in-house counsel for Qualtrics International,
bestselling author, *Hail Mary:*
The Inside Story of BYU's 1980 Miracle Bowl Comeback

"*Authentic Strengths* is downright elucidative when it comes to enabling people to lead more fulfilling lives through a plethora of concepts, research and exercises split into three major sections: *Explore your strengths, Empower your strengths,* and *Engage your strengths.* The reader will discover a set of tools aimed at evoking one's inner coach, nurturing one's personal and professional strengths, and flourishing to a whole and sustainably productive life. This welcome experience-based book contributes to the fields of positive psychology, as well as personal and professional leadership."

—**Flora Victoria,** President of SBCoaching© Empresas, Brasil

"Valuable insights! Tremendous information and practical application that focuses on the core values of people—their character strengths. An excellent guide that enables us to coach our clients to utilize their best qualities and achieve their professional and personal goals. This excellent coaching book will enrich human performance and influence well-being; and it can also be applied beyond cultural boundaries—even in a dynamic society like Southeast Asia."

—**Character Plus Co., Ltd.,** – Thailand

"This book is a necessary read for practitioners, educators and parents—anyone wanting to help others explore their own strengths and truly capitalize on the value of individuals. We become better leaders and parents as we learn skills to empower ourselves with a greater understanding of our children, coworkers and students. Our influence will grow as we utilize the principles in this book to better relate to each other through the lens of strengths. Doman provides fresh insight and practical application that gives clarity to the science behind positive psychology. Each chapter is personally and professionally inspiring."

—**Dr. Jaynee Poulson**, Utah State PTA Health Commissioner, Professor at Weber State University, Former CEO, The Life House Counseling Center

"Authentic and genuine! Doman combines personal stories and coaching case studies in a powerful way to illustrate the concepts she is teaching. This is a must-read for all of those who use positive psychology in their coaching or mental health practices or for those who are just trying to implement positive psychological concepts in their own lives. Fatima shows us how to create and use a 'strengths fingerprint' in our personal lives as well as our work. I love the main message of this book of changing 'what's wrong to what's strong.' I will certainly recommend this to all of my students and patients."

—**Trish Henrie-Barrus**, Ph.D.; President & Founder, InteraSolutions; Assistant Professor in the Department of Educational Psychology & Developer for the Positive Psychology Certificate Program, University of Utah; Owner, Riverwoods Behavioral Health

"A brilliant contribution to positive psychology and executive coaching! This book is a must-read for anyone wanting to bring out what is best in themselves, their relationships and their work. The author takes us on a fascinating journey of self-discovery and empowerment by focusing on our most precious gift—our character strengths. Fatima Doman has given us a wonderful compass by which we can navigate toward a flourishing life!"

—**Dr. Lucia Ceja**, CEO and Co-founder, Sparkling Strategies SL, Spain

"Fatima Doman masterfully outlines a practical step-by-step method for strengths coaching and individuals interested in self-coaching. Doman supports the claim that deploying character strengths such as gratitude, perseverance, forgiveness, hope, and other positive mental states enhances life satisfaction, reduces unhealthy negativity, and fosters the type of enduring happiness that comes from finding meaning and a purpose beyond oneself."

—**J. Goodman Farr**, M.Ed.; Counselor, Educator, and Wellness Trainer; Founder, Positive Psychology Program and Applied Positive Psychology undergraduate certificate program, University of Utah

"The next step in bringing out the best in people. A coaching book that teaches you the core principles of positive psychology needed to enable people to flourish. It brings a totally new perspective on individual and team coaching by a truly great trainer and coach. This book is for everyone who wants to live a positive, productive and meaningful life."

—**Edwin Boom**, CEO and Founder, MOOVS Training Company, Netherlands

"I have been teaching principles of personal leadership to college students for fifteen years, and the single most significant aspect I try to facilitate in students is to get them to challenge their existing habits of mind so they can tap into their best selves. Fatima Doman's book masterfully converges with what we teach. Applying the concepts in this book will generate outcomes of heightened awareness, synergistic results, and interdependent behaviors that we all desire. It is my hope that someday universities will offer a class dedicated to strengths so that we can take the *Authentic Strengths* vision and make it a reality."

—**Denise Richards, MBA**, Associate Professor, Department of Student Leadership and Success Studies, Utah Valley University

"Written out of more than two decades of experience successfully coaching and training leaders around the world, Doman's new book, *Authentic Strengths*, lays out evidence-based, highly accessible, and personally transformative strategies for coaching. The all-important learning of becoming authentic includes first accepting responsibility for oneself, and then stepping onto the path of self-awareness and self-acceptance. I am thrilled about the possibilities for integrating Doman's approach into the First Year Experience university courses I teach, and for authentic strengths to become a game changer for students!"

—**Lisa Lambert, MBA**, Department of Student Leadership and Success Studies, Utah Valley University

"A significant contribution to the fields of coaching and applied positive psychology. Fatima Doman provides an accessible framework for coaching one's self and others to maximize potential—personally and professionally. Cutting edge coaching for the 21st century!"

—**Talyaa Vardar**, MA, PCC, Academic Director, Flow Coaching International, Turkey

AUTHENTIC STRENGTHS

AUTHENTIC STRENGTHS

Maximize Your Happiness, Performance & Success with Positive Psychology Coaching

Fatima Doman

NEXT CENTURY
PUBLISHING

Authentic Strengths
Maximize Your Happiness, Performance & Success with Positive Psychology Coaching

Published by Next Century Publishing
Las Vegas, Nevada
www.NextCenturyPublishing.com

ISBN: 978-1-68102-083-9
Library of Congress Control Number: 2015951899

Printed in the United States of America

Disclaimer
The information presented in this book is the result of years of practical experience and research. This content is of a general nature and not a substitute for an evaluation or treatment by a competent professional or medical practitioner. If you believe you are in need of psychological or physical interventions, please see a practitioner as soon as possible. The book's author cannot guarantee results—neither expressed nor implied.

For my sons

KADEN AND SAGE —

You inspire me every day to learn and grow.

TABLE OF CONTENTS

AUTHENTIC STRENGTHS

PREFACE

By Dr. Neal H. Mayerson

Founder and Chairman of the VIA Institute on Character

As a clinical psychologist who has spent thousands of hours with people helping them improve their lives, and as founder and chairman of the VIA Institute and owner of a coaching company that trained and hired coaches, I was elated to learn that my friend and colleague Fatima Doman decided to write this book. Coaching is a rapidly expanding practice field, yet there are few universities with standardized training and credentialing programs. As a result, coaches choose from varied alternatives to obtain training and pursue ongoing learning. The science-based coaching process described in this book will soon be at the vanguard for establishing coaching excellence.

Many books, workshops, and training programs for coaching have taken note of the relatively new area of social science called positive psychology. And, most of these make reference to being "strength-based." However, this book is the first of its kind that focuses deeply and meaningfully on character strengths. Character strengths are important positive aspects of our identity and personality. They define what's best about each of us and represent a set of powerful tools that each of us can use to become best versions of ourselves and to help others do the same. They can be distinguished from strengths of talent. While the latter define what we are good at doing, character strengths define what we *care* about doing.

Helping clients bring into focus who they are in terms of positive personality inclinations is fundamental to empowering them to become architects of their own lives. Knowing what dimensions of ourselves are most important to express and be known for becomes the compass by which we can navigate so many of life's decisions—from what kinds of work and activities we will find most fulfilling, to who we want to be in relationship with and how we want to relate to others. Finally, now, with the publication of this book, coaches and leaders can learn an approach to coaching that builds upon people's most important assets—their character strengths. This book takes what other books only make marginal reference to and brings it front and center to where it belongs in effective coaching. With deep expertise Ms. Doman unpacks theory and science into useable and practical insights for practitioners and anyone wanting to be a better coach to himself or others.

I hope each reader will give this book his undivided attention and will think deeply about how to take what is learned here and apply it to his personalized approach to coaching others, as well as himself, to well-being.

FOREWORD

By Dr. Terrence E. Maltbia

Founder and Faculty Director of the Columbia University
Coaching Certification Program

Dr. Mayerson's preface clearly lays out the value of this book, predicting it will soon be "at the vanguard of establishing coaching excellence"—I could not agree more! As the Founder and Faculty Director of Columbia University's Coaching Certification Program, our ongoing exploration of existing, coaching-specific research, currently available to support the rapidly growing professional practice of executive and organizational coaching, reveals it's limited at best. Fatima Doman was a member of our program's first cohort in 2007, where during the field-based practicum her coach-specific research project had a decidedly "strengths-based" focus. It is gratifying to witness the culmination of that early work resulting in this book that is both practical, yet grounded in relevant science.

Specifically, in this three-part book professional coaches, coach educators and supervisors, as well as organizational leaders and individuals are guided through a clear blueprint for explicitly leveraging the power of coaching in service of realizing superior results and enhanced human performance. In Part I: Explore, Doman provides the foundation for exploring one's strengths grounded in twenty four evidence-based character strengths found to contribute to well-being and performance! The ideas outlined in the chapters that makeup this part of the book are essential for the positive coach-client growth mindset and alignment of expectations for optimum results.

In Part II: Empower, Doman focuses on leveraging increased awareness of one's character strengths as a source of motivation and empowerment. The chapters in this section brilliantly introduce practical structures and tools for tapping into the sources of one's motivation; reframing "perceived failures" as a platform for learning, growth and forward momentum; and importing strategies for bringing a mindful approach to regulation of emotions, especially in situations involving stress.

Finally, in Part III: Engage, Doman masterfully combines the work of exploring one's character strengths and using increased awareness of strengths as a source of empowerment to the important work of taking informed action—engaging one's strengths to live a fulfilling life while achieving the results one truly desires. Here she makes distinctions between emotional competence (including character strengths), which can be learned, and IQ, which tends to be a more stable characteristic.

As an organizational leader, educator, researcher, executive coach, and consultant with more than thirty years of experience, I found Ms. Doman's ability to integrate theory, research and practice impressive, relevant and an important contribution to the emerging field of executive and organizational coaching! It is my hope that each reader gains the insights I've gained. I will add this to the set of core resources that guide my professional coaching practice. Congratulations, Fatima on a job well done! Two thumbs up!

If we all did what
we are capable
of doing, we
would literally
ASTOUND
ourselves.

Thomas Edison

INTRODUCTION

Jewelers spot diamonds in the rough. Art dealers identify potential masterpieces. Coaches groom stars. If you have picked up this book, you are on your way to being a star performer. You have acknowledged your motivation to reach a new level of potential. How can individuals discover their character strengths and ignite their greatest potential? One way is to have it reflected back to them by someone who can see clearly what has been obscured by layers of non-constructive feedback, misguided efforts, and the wrong focus.

Drawing on the best from the science of positive psychology and from my two decades of experience coaching others both in my own company, Authentic Strengths Advantage® and previously with the world's largest leadership training company, I have created a strengths coaching process based on timeless, powerful principles that can transform a dedicated learner into a coach par excellence. The strengths coaching process you will learn in this book applies whether you lead others or simply want to increase your own personal effectiveness. During my twenty years with FranklinCovey, we worked with ninety percent of the Fortune 100 companies and eighty percent of the Fortune 500 companies. The company trained more than 250,000 people each month within organizations across 135 countries and 45 global offices. I have worked with thousands of leaders in organizations worldwide and have gained significant insights as we worked through their biggest challenges.

My later work with the Columbia University Coaching Certification Program and the VIA Institute on Character propelled me to better understand what really motivates people to achieve their goals. This book results from my careful study of what ignites star performance and my own experiences witnessing astonishing transformational change in the people I have coached. Throughout these pages I have changed names and identifying features to preserve confidentiality in the coaching stories I share with you.

What Is Strengths Coaching?

Why do I believe strengths coaching has emerged as such an important vehicle for discovering and unleashing potential? While coaching and training executives in personal development, productivity and leadership content, I regularly pondered how to empower people to create sustainable, positive change. One of the most intensive work production studies in history (over 10 years of research and 200,000 interviews) by Towers Watson research firm expands on the groundbreaking "Hawthorne Effect" studies of the 1950s, which showed that people tend to work harder and perform better when they are observed. Simply put, when you pay attention to the uniqueness in people, they light up. All you have to do is look at how babies respond to the personal attention and positive feedback that is commonly given to the miracle of a new life. Why do we stop nourishing each other with attention as if we are less miraculous just because we become independent adults?

> Simply put, when you pay attention to the uniqueness in people, they light up.

A subsequent 2012 Towers Watson Global Workforce Study listed top motivators for employee engagement designed for the twenty-first century workplace. Among them we find leadership assigning tasks that are suited to employees' strengths and showing sincere interest in employees' well-being and earning employees' trust and confidence.[1] Their study of over 32,000 employees showed that anxiety about the future is common throughout the world and only 35 percent of the global workforce is highly engaged. Positive psychology research is showing that strengths-focused coaching creates a more optimistic and solution-focused outlook in people. Appreciating and leveraging employee strengths, while creating a culture of mutual respect where people are empowered to make their unique contributions is key to motivating and engaging people.

Indeed, extensive research into human behavior and strengths by Gallup backs up the Towers Watson findings. People who use their strengths every day are six times more likely to be engaged on the job, and employers that focus on employees' strengths rather than focusing on correcting their weaknesses have a far more engaged workforce.

To measure corporate success at focusing on employees' strengths, Gallup developed the Strengths Orientation Index, which asks employees about how their employers do on four key items:

1. Every week, goals and expectations are set based on employee strengths.

2. Employees can name the strengths of five people with whom they work.

3. Supervisors have meaningful discussions about strengths with employees.

4. The organization is committed to building the strengths of each employee.

Shockingly, only three percent of employees of the U.S. based companies surveyed could strongly agree with all four of the Strengths Orientation Index items. This low agreement level demonstrates that the vast number of employers are failing to accentuate the positive and are making the costly mistake of spending valuable resources on attempts to address employees' weaknesses. Yet the survey results demonstrated that employees reward strengths-focused employers with greater effort, a stronger work ethic, increased commitment and more enthusiasm.

One study asked 1,003 employees about their supervisors' approach to their strengths vs. weaknesses or whether they felt ignored entirely. Of the thirty-seven percent who felt their supervisors focused on their strengths, disengagement fell to just one percent! And among that thirty-seven percent getting kudos from bosses for their strong suits, nearly two-thirds (sixty-one percent) were engaged in their workplaces. That's twice the average of U.S. workers who are engaged nationwide.

Engaged employees who feel their strengths are well utilized are significantly more productive, less stressed, make fewer mistakes and create higher quality work. They take fewer sick days and experience fewer chronic health problems—all of which leads to a healthier bottom line.[2] The jaw-dropping numbers generated by strengths research prove that a strengths focus paves the way to success, fulfillment, and improved performance.

So why, after all the years of research emphasizing over and over again the huge benefit of focusing on strengths rather than weaknesses, does virtually every organization direct a laser-like focus on weaknesses? In many countries, it starts in schools, where the focus is too often on weaknesses rather than identifying and nurturing strengths. In fact, many of us do not know how to identify our own character strengths—much less someone else's. Since so much attention is heaped on our weaknesses, we are often unaware of our strengths. Because we are wired to survive, human beings have tended to focus on what's wrong (our and others' weaknesses). But the time has come to rewire our minds to thrive and to shift our focus to what's strong (our strengths).

> **Strengths coaching affirms our untapped potential rather than the limits of what we can do.**

Strengths coaching affirms our untapped potential rather than the limits of what we can do. The job of a strengths coach is to amplify, reflect and facilitate strengths, while generating strategies and solutions for the person being coached. My practical experience has taught me that adhering to strengths coaching principles and practicing coaching presence—being fully present with someone in the moment—matter more than technique and style. A great coach gathers information by listening for emotion in addition to just hearing the words being said, all the while attending carefully to visual cues. Effective coaches pick up cues even from micro-expressions—that flicker of unguarded expression that flashes across a person's face and communicates important information to those attuned to it. When a gifted coach connects with a person in this way, deep communication results. Amazing results await anyone who dares to push ego aside and lead from a place of genuine desire to help another discover and reach his potential. Discovering and unleashing potential is a matter of helping individuals get in touch with and give voice to their inner coach, the authentic part of themselves. That voice is the most powerful guide we each have for leading us to our personal best.

A 2014 International Coach Federation (ICF) Global Awareness Study of over 18,000 people worldwide showed that among those who would consider coaching, the most frequently cited motivations were defining their own strengths and weaknesses (forty-seven percent), followed by a desire to maximize their own potential (forty-one percent).[3] This leading motivation for coaching centered on exploring one's strengths and unleashing one's potential is why I created the Authentic Strengths Advantage® coaching process.

What Is the Authentic Strengths Advantage®?

I define the Authentic Strengths Advantage® as a process of helping people connect to their authentic passion and purpose—their personal contribution to the world. This personal contribution is ignited to full flame when we tap into our strengths, that core part of ourselves that energizes us and gives life its savor. Inherent in every individual is the potential for greatness. As a member of the International Coach Federation, I echo ICF's core belief that people are "naturally creative, resourceful, and whole." When you put strengths coaching into practice, you are acknowledging that the person being coached intuitively has the answers and solutions within herself or himself.

> **The best leaders and coaches know how to inspire and allow people to bring their authentic selves to work, creating the conditions for a sustainable high performance.**

A strengths coach's job isn't to impose his or her own opinion, will, or even well-meaning intentions on another. Rather, the best leaders and coaches know how to inspire and allow people to bring their authentic selves to work, creating the conditions for sustainable high performance. Authenticity is central to strengths coaching because it is the key to fully engaging people to make a distinctive and meaningful contribution not just at work, but also in the many facets of their personal lives.

I recently gave a strengths presentation to one of the largest law enforcement departments in the United States. I had been warned not to expect much interaction or buy-in from the scores of captains and lieutenants in attendance. The training leader said, "Don't let them intimidate you, Fatima. You will probably be looking at a lot of blank, stoic faces; and they may even be openly hostile to positive psychology. Don't expect them to talk much."

What I encountered was the opposite. When we discussed that the law enforcement profession carries with it some of the highest suicide, divorce and spousal abuse rates of any profession, they were eager for a panacea for their problems. The challenge, they told me, is that to survive on the streets you have to be extremely fast and adept at following highly skilled training in the moment. What if they could also train for resiliency and develop the ability to come down off the adrenaline rush faster to a place of emotional and mental clarity? What if they could develop the very strengths that are shown to counteract post-traumatic stress? They were so energized by the skills and tools of the strengths training that I introduced that I often could not get them to stop talking in their groups long enough to move on to the next topic!

One of the captains came up to me after the training and said he would like to see character strengths training taken to the prison system. He said, "Could you imagine the impact if we provided this information to each new inmate? Most of them have probably never had anyone help them identify their character strengths, let alone had much positive feedback, ever."

In this book, I offer a practical, three-step process that will take your life and the lives of those you influence in fulfilling directions beyond your expectations. Through this process, you will explore your character strengths, see how strengths have enabled prior success and learn how to recreate success at will. You will empower the use of your strengths personally and professionally with sustainable motivation and set goals empowered by strengths. Finally, you will engage your character strengths using a weekly process based on the principle of positive progression—all the while honoring the strengths in others.

ENGAGE
Strengths in Action
Reflect, Reveal, Recalibrate/CSQ

EMPOWER
Strengths Motivation
Feedback/Feed Forward
Motivation Grid/STRONG Goals

EXPLORE
Strengths Awareness
Life Sketch/Whole Life Scale
Best Self/STRONG Filter/STRONG Thoughts

CHARACTER STRENGTHS

The Significance of Coaching

Coaches have empowered the success of others since the beginning of time. Tribal elders were revered for their wisdom and consulted for guidance. Nations' forefathers and founding mothers established standards for civilization. And throughout the ages, most people would name their parents and grandparents as their best coaches. As both nuclear and extended family and support structures have broken down, finding a wise coach has become more challenging, yet even more important to those who want to excel.

We all face setbacks and personal challenges. Learning from failure is as much a part of greatness as success. How you rebound and grow is what makes the difference. The watchful eye and keen perspective of a strengths coach offers a sustainable edge to enhancing performance—reflecting back the unique strengths within the person being coached and inspiring the use of character strengths in new, often surprising and better ways.

A coach's most important job is to offer encouragement—which comes from the Latin word *cor*, meaning "heart"—or to hearten and inspire. Think about that for a moment. What a gift to know that the most important job you can take on is being an encourager to yourself and to all those around you.

No one reaches the top without being led or carried part of the way. Whether you are coaching yourself, being coached or learning to coach others, strengths coaching brings out the best in you, your significant other, your child, your employee, your team, your boss, your organization—in anyone and everyone you seek to positively influence.

Your coach,

Fatima Doman

Part I | EXPLORE YOUR STRENGTHS

"We are each gifted in a unique and important way. It is our privilege and our adventure to discover our own special light."

—Mary Dunbar

"Any transformational process begins with self-awareness—knowing oneself. In the explore stage of strengths coaching we visit the past briefly for context to better understand previous life patterns and how strengths have enabled prior success. But the goal of strengths coaching is to move quickly into the present where the work of growth takes place, and to learn to recreate success at will—all the while clearly defining our vision of our ideal 'whole life' future powered by our strengths."

—Fatima Doman

ENGAGE
Strengths in Action
Reflect, Reveal, Recalibrate/CSQ

EMPOWER
Strengths Motivation
Feedback/Feed Forward
Motivation Grid/STRONG Goals

EXPLORE
Strengths Awareness
Life Sketch/Whole Life Scale
Best Self/STRONG Filter/STRONG Thoughts

CHARACTER STRENGTHS

If you stop to give the devil a ride, he is eventually going to want to DRIVE

Folk saying

1 | SILENCE THE CRITIC, DISCOVER THE COACH

"Changing the destructive things you say to yourself when you experience the setbacks that life deals all of us is the central skill of optimism."

—Dr. Martin E. P. Seligman

"If you hear a voice within you say 'you cannot paint,' then by all means paint and that voice will be silenced."

—Vincent Van Gogh

Consider a top-performing concert musician who, in her quest for perfection, is painfully self-critical each time she makes a mistake. Is that internal, criticizing voice the key to her success? What if there was a better, more sustainable way to bring out the same or an even higher level of excellence? What if the key to unleashing greatness is to silence the inner critic and instead discover the inner coach?

I was deeply moved as I witnessed a powerful coaching demonstration by Benjamin Zander at a Harvard Medical School positive psychology coaching conference. Ben, conductor of the Boston Philharmonic, had brought an amazing string quartet to the event. When the newest member of the quartet made a mistake, Ben made the musicians stop in the middle of the piece they were playing. The errant violinist's expression was excruciating as she hit herself on the top of her head in frustration.

"I need you to stand and throw your arms up in the air and say 'How fascinating!'" Ben good naturedly prompted the musician. For a moment she wavered, looking at him quizzically. She did as commanded tentatively. "Good," he said. "Now try it again." He instructed her to repeat the words and the act of throwing up her arms. Eventually she was smiling broadly and was once again relaxed enough to carry on with the performance.

Rather than making a mistake an occasion for fear and humiliation, Ben welcomed it with exuberance, neutralizing the shame. He was making an unforgettable point for those of us in attendance. As I sat enraptured not only by the music, but also by the experience of witnessing how a mistake could be viewed as a "fascinating" opportunity for learning, I was filled with emotion. You could feel the release in the spirits of the musicians as they gave themselves wholeheartedly to the music, which was full of enthusiasm when it continued. It was as if the notes and movement had more syntax than I had ever experienced. Removing negative thinking from a traditionally embarrassing experience was transformative for both the musicians and the audience.

Witnessing how Ben reframed the negative opened up something new for me. I had come to the conference feeling disappointed about a work experience. It wasn't all that significant—I had just inadvertently left the wrong date on my "I'll be out of the office" message. A colleague with a critical eye emailed another colleague with a snide remark about the slip. This was someone I had wanted to work with on a project, so I beat myself up for not catching the error, for not being perfect.

After Ben's thought-provoking presentation, I reflected, "What can I learn about myself from this work incident?" I pondered for a few moments and decided: I can go slower and take the time to proof my work. I can develop a thicker skin and focus on what is important to me, not on someone else's negative comment. I can harbor no ill will and not let it eat away at me. I can say, "How fascinating!"

As I sat in my chair watching Ben turn a mistake into a growth experience, my frustration about my own performance dropped away. My heart felt lighter. My own inner critic's voice was silenced—and in the silence, I could hear what I needed to hear: Celebrate the victory of not putting yourself down. "That is a big win," my inner coach told me. "You are off the bench and in the game."

If we're going to talk to ourselves about what we have done, why not be encouraging instead of punitive? Why not compliment our progress instead of picking apart our *faux pas*? The challenge is to grow from our mistakes instead of letting them shrink us. I left that string quartet performance feeling that I, too, could make beautiful music, playing with a passion I had never felt before in my own arena of work. Not that we want to make mistakes, but I learned I can reach for my highest level of performance without the fear of failure, because failure can be an opportunity to learn and grow. You never know when a setback could put you ahead. That's living in the realm of possibility rather than in an arena with a penalty box.

> **Star performers understand the importance of using objective, creative, solution-oriented, and encouraging self-talk.**

Star performers understand the importance of using objective, creative, solution-oriented, and encouraging self-talk. When we use negative, blaming, or self-deprecating language, in essence we're saying that we're victims—that we do not influence our own destiny. When we obsessively think about all the things causing us stress, we override our creative options to influence our situation. Consequently, we have less time and energy to spend on the very things that will change our situation for the better. Even if your creative bandwidth appears small, I strongly encourage you to stay focused on it. What you focus on grows, and little by little, it will expand. You will surprise yourself with your increased options.

Check Your Mindset: Coach vs. Critic

I was exposed to a powerful thinking model during my Columbia University Coaching Certification Program. I adapted it as a tool for my coaching clients, and I have named it the Coach/Critic Model. It helps coaches define thinking style, behavior, and outcomes. Coaches can use it to help themselves improve their coaching style or have people they coach use it to better understand how they view themselves, and how they show up in personal and professional relationships. Another use is to introduce the model while coaching teams to promote a positive work environment. The model is a tool to clarify whether and how much one is operating as a Coach or a Critic. The goal, of course, is to increase the time spent on the Coach side. I ask my clients to stand as they read each column of words and to notice the difference in how their bodies feel/respond to words characterizing each thinking style. I am consistently impressed with the insights this simple activity evokes for my clients. Without fail they report discernable physical, mental, and emotional manifestations depending on the words they are reading. It is not surprising that positive psychology research is showing similar mind-body correlations to language and thought patterns.

Inner Critic	Inner Coach
Weakness focus	Strengths focus
Problem-oriented	Solution-oriented
Fixed mindset	Growth mindset
Blame/Judge	Learn
Disregard	Respect
Know it already	Curious
Afraid of change	Open to change
Either/or thinking	Creative thinking
Use "but"	Use "and"
Looks for offense	Looks for intent

Coach/Critic Model, © 2014 Authentic Strengths Advantage. (Adapted from Columbia University Coaching Certification Program Learner/Judger Model. Source: Marilee C. Goldberg's, The Art of the Question 1998 p. 161-178)

Critic Relationship	Coach Relationship
Competitive	Cooperative
Individualistic	Teamwork
Threatened by differences	Values differences
Defensive	Dialogue/feedback
Entrenched	Seeks common ground
Afraid of change	Dynamic, growing

Coach/Critic Model, © 2014 Authentic Strengths Advantage. (Adapted from Columbia University Coaching Certification Program Learner/Judger Model. Source: Marilee C. Goldberg's, *The Art of the Question* 1998 p. 161-178)

The Critic: Saboteur of Creativity

Musicians are notorious for being self-critical. According to a survey reported in an article in *The Music Quarterly*, musicians in seventy-eight American, British, and German orchestras rated their job satisfaction lower than that of prison guards.[1]

Ben Zander's positive approach to coaching musicians boosted audience attendance as well as the satisfaction of his orchestra members, among other positive effects. Turning a wrong note, a traditionally humiliating experience, into a celebration of learning silenced the critic and gave voice to the inner coach words to defuse negative feelings. This enabled a positive approach to a common challenge for a musician. His action took the paralyzing shame, fear, and negativity out of the picture and put the experience on a different playing field—one in which we accept mistakes as part of the learning process. A significant by-product of showing interest in examining a mistake without blame is that we probably won't make that particular mistake again.

Rather than risk the joy being sucked out of playing music, Ben decided to assume he was working with phenomenal musicians, every one of whom had already earned an A. In fact, he told us his first assignment to all his students is to write a paper on how they will have earned an A by the end of the course. He requires all his students to raise their arms in the air and say "How fascinating!" when they don't perform flawlessly.

Try it. The jab of the critic, whose constant judgment is about as helpful as a poke in the eye, will immediately be intercepted and deflected. Incidentally, the Boston Philharmonic sells out performance after performance at a time when other orchestras are going bankrupt. Could the overwhelming patronage be due to the joy and confidence that comes across in the music?

Once you open the door for your inner critic, you are essentially giving your keys to a driver whose judgment you may not agree with. The critic can hijack you and take you to places you never intended to end up. It can be a dangerous ride.

Negative Thoughts Constrict

The inner coach is the opposite of the inner critic. Thoughts that bring about despair or discouragement become obnoxiously loud, drowning out your inner coach and preventing your character strengths from expressing themselves. A sincere desire to change and become better is very different from the feeling of despair or discouragement, which paralyzes us. Negative thoughts are lies that sabotage, drain and upset you. If you suffer from those feelings, it's a signal that your inner critic is directing the action.

> A sincere desire to change and become better is very different from the feeling of despair or discouragement, which paralyzes us.

Aaron Beck, the father of cognitive therapy, began helping patients identify and evaluate negative thoughts. He found that by doing so, patients were able to think more realistically. This in turn led them to feel better emotionally and behave more functionally. He discovered that distorted thinking has a negative effect on our emotional state and behavior. Beck helped people become aware of their distorted thinking and taught them how to challenge its effects. Your inner critic thrives on distorted and inaccurate thinking such as catastrophizing ("this project is doomed to failure"), all-or-nothing thinking ("she never responds/always responds that way to my emails"), or discounting positive experiences ("he only helped on that project because he wanted the credit").

Spread Your Wings and Fly

One of my clients had struggled with stress-related health challenges, including such intense anxiety that her doctor outfitted her with a heart monitor on two occasions and suggested that she seek stress-management coaching. A devoted wife and mother who leads a non-profit organization in Europe, she is a high achiever and role model for others. This woman was plagued by fears and doubts that caused such intense distress that she would be incapacitated for hours or even a whole day at a time.

In one of our first sessions, she briefly shared with me memories of her childhood that she thought might be skewing her adult perspective. She was raised in a loving home but was surrounded by illness and excessive worry. She watched a family member struggle through a terminal illness from his birth until his premature death in his twenties.

She was suffering on three fronts: her inner critic was so loud she couldn't hear anything else, the resulting negative state silenced her inner coach who would otherwise have been able to guide her out of such distress, and her head was filled with persistent, debilitating thoughts—she was stuck in fearful rumination.

After practicing positive, inner coach, affirming self-talk—encouraging thoughts and phrases—during periods of anxiety, her inner critic lost some of its power. She began to come up with evidence based on her important work with a nonprofit organization to counter the inner critic telling her she was a failure. The more light she shed on her fears, bringing them into the open, the more they scattered. This allowed her to focus on replacing the negative thoughts with objective thoughts grounded in reality.

She began retraining her thinking patterns to focus on the positive and rein in her irrational fears and negative thinking. She used the calming act of breathing exercises in times of stress and made a habit of reading something inspiring to start every morning. She felt so much safer that every aspect of her life dramatically improved. Her stomach problems and

> I choose to spread my wings and fly like a beautiful butterfly.

headaches subsided. She had a shift of perspective that freed her to live fearlessly. She discovered that because she had felt fear, she could now recognize courage.

In a note to me she said that what she learned during her coaching experience was how to conquer her obsessive worrying. She recognized that she always has a choice, and one of those is to be, as we had discussed in coaching, a "positive, creative solver." She was relieved that coaching was not about finding blame with parents or past circumstances, but rather about taking initiative to create a new and better tomorrow. She found out that faith in a better future requires action—you can't just say you have faith; you have to act on it. "I choose to spread my wings and fly like a beautiful butterfly," she wrote, "instead of curling up and hiding like a potato bug."

When you learn to recognize a debilitating negative thought trying to sabotage hopeful inner coach thoughts, turn it away immediately. Counter critical thoughts by thinking of all the objective reasons you should reject them, or by saying to yourself, "That simply isn't true."

Welcoming the Positive

Jewish psychiatrist and Holocaust survivor Viktor Frankl, under the most difficult circumstances imaginable, used the ability only humans possess: to choose his own thoughts to create a meaningful personal vision in the midst of hellish chaos. He liberated himself to live fully—long before the Americans marched in.

While in four Nazi death camps, including Auschwitz, he chose to base his behavior and values on his own self-awareness rather than to react to how he was defined by his captors. He saw himself lecturing to his future students about the lessons he was learning daily, using his innate power to exercise his options, which inspired and unleashed human potential in others as well.

In his own words: "We who lived in the concentration camps can remember the men who walked through the huts comforting others, giving away their last piece of bread. They may have been few in number, but they offer sufficient proof that everything can be taken from a man but one thing: the last of the human freedoms—to choose one's attitude in any given set of circumstances, to choose one's own way."[2] He was in effect calling forth his inner coach who successfully silenced the saboteur.

When we choose to listen to our inner coach who evokes our best self, we inspire both ourselves and others to be more resourceful and creative. Our best self is at risk of getting lost in the chaotic noise of everyday life. In order to identify the best path through life's distractions, we must acquire the skill of giving voice to our inner coach.

Conversely, when we choose to be a victim, listening to our inner critic who devalues our beliefs, attacks our self-worth, and blocks our initiative, we give away our stabilizing, self-motivating inner power. Fortunately we can retrain our thinking to notice our character strengths and to appreciate the best in ourselves and in each moment.

The Benefits of Strengths Coaching

When social scientists examined the effects of strengths coaching, they found important benefits. A strengths coach:

- Looks through the lens of strengths before addressing challenges
- Creates safety while discussing difficult issues, instilling confidence and hope
- Actively listens and takes time to fully understand
- Enables strengths awareness and insights
- Challenges you to find your best answers
- Guides you through strengths-focused goal setting
- Focuses on present/future aspirations and holds you accountable to the strengths goals you have set

When people utilized these benefits, self-reflection decreased while insight increased. In other words, less self-focused rumination led to better self-regulation of goals, and that led to better mental health, quality of life, and general satisfaction.[3]

Another study showed that solution-focused coaching enhanced goal striving, well-being, and hope; and gains were maintained thirty weeks after the conclusion of the intervention.[4]

Transformation Powered by Questions

Many of life's toughest issues are not solved by having all the answers, but rather by asking the right questions. Coaches who ask powerful and provocative questions help individuals and teams gain real clarity, purpose, and insight. Ongoing questioning, self-assessment, and feedback are all part of the vital process for learning, growth, development, and performance improvement.

The nature of the questions matter, too. In a study by Grant and O'Connor, the impact of solution-focused questions versus problem-focused coaching questions was explored.[5] Although both enhanced the participants' goal attainment, the solution-focused group experienced much better results. Participants were more energized and motivated by the positivity of the questions.

Examples of solution-focused questions:

- Imagine the solution to your issue had somehow come about. What does the solution look like?

- What are some ways you could start to move toward creating this solution?

- What impact is thinking about this solution having on you?

Examples of problem-focused questions:

- How long has this been a problem? How did it start?

- What are your thoughts about this problem?

- What impact is thinking about this problem having on you?

Whether you are coaching yourself or others, your job as a strengths coach is simple: Ask open-ended, solution-oriented questions about how, what, when, etc. Open-ended questions, which have no fixed answers, allow you to get to both the content of what has happened, and how the person being coached is feeling or responding to the situation. Listening will help you uncover truth as the person is experiencing it. Asking open-ended questions lets the person you are coaching tell the storyline, the situation, and his or her reaction to it. Encourage the person not just to state or think about hopeful solutions, but also to try to *feel* the effects of the solutions, thereby empowering the solutions with added motivation.[6]

At the end of each chapter, I've included a few examples of the kind of coaching questions I use in my coaching practice. Since the strengths coaching questions I use are rooted in positive psychology and are designed to build mental and emotional strength, I call them "STRONG Questions©." Studies show that the best way to anchor what you are learning is to teach it to someone else within a day or so, while it is still fresh in your mind. If you want to internalize the insights you've learned in each chapter of this book, find someone—a coworker, a friend, a family member—and share what you've learned with him or her. Ask yourself the thought-provoking "STRONG Questions©." Then try using them in a coaching situation.

Solution-oriented questions are one of the most powerful tools you have at your disposal. The right question can unlock a wealth of understanding and unleash a world of potential.

Coaching Tip

The STRONG Questions© at the end of each chapter will help you apply the coaching principles discussed in the chapter. Use the questions below to determine whether you are listening to your inner coach or your inner critic.

STRONG Questions©: Mindset

- What "fascinating" thing can I learn from this challenging experience?

- What are the facts in this situation? What actually happened?

- What exact words were said and what actions took place, without my interpretation?

- What did I make up/interpret about the situation? Is my interpretation completely accurate?

- What did I learn that changed my view of the situation?

- How did this new perspective shift my behavior?

- Am I using inner coach or inner critic language?

- Who and what am I empowering?

- What is a better, coach-oriented way to respond?

- What would be the positive outcomes of responding in this new way?

- What are some things I could begin doing today to bring about these changes?

In essence, coaches shift attention from what causes and drives pain to what energizes and pulls people forward. They follow the

T R A I L
of
DREAMS

Dr. Carol Kauffman

2 | MOVE FROM WHAT'S WRONG TO WHAT'S STRONG

"Character Strengths are the fuel and the rudder that propel our talents and give them direction."

—Dr. Neal H. Mayerson

Imagine you found a flower bud in your garden—you see the bud, but are unsure what flower will unfold from it. If you have a predetermined wish or requirement for it to be one vs. another, such as wanting an orchid to be a geranium or a tulip to be a rose, you will be disappointed when the "wrong" one unfolds. You will focus on what's wrong with it and try to make it what you want it to be, and in so doing you will harm it and prevent it from reaching its potential. It will wither.

Unfortunately, the world is full of withered and withering people, because others around them have neither respected and nurtured their innate character nor valued their uniqueness. Often the loud inner critic joins in the game by squashing a person's authenticity and trying to mold him into some preconceived ideal.

Martin Seligman, Ph.D., the father of the positive psychology movement, explained in his groundbreaking books, *Authentic Happiness,* and *Flourish,*[1] that once we know what our best qualities are, they open up a vital pathway to engagement—at work, in relationships and in life. Due to the new science of positive psychology (which focuses on what's right about a person) vs. the old problem-focused approach, we now can help people identify the character strengths that define who they are at their best. The qualities that, when nurtured, can lead to good outcomes in every area of their lives.

The VIA Survey of Character Strengths is a scientifically valid, peer-reviewed tool. It helps people to focus on "what's strong" (their strengths), instead of "what's wrong" (their weaknesses). For example, the survey might show a person's top character strengths as being qualities like leadership, kindness and creativity. (You will find information at the end of this chapter about where to access this free survey.)

As two decades of research in the field of positive psychology and hundreds of studies have now shown, people who express their strengths more tend to be happier, more engaged, energetic, resilient, less stressed and higher achievers.

To fully understand why character strengths are so important, we need to first understand what human beings want. Human beings have some fundamental needs that include expressing who we are, being recognized/valued/accepted by others, and feeling part of something bigger than ourselves. These are basic nutrients that nourish the human psyche. The workplace is a perfect setting to get these needs met—to be our best version of ourselves, to recognize and to be recognized and to be part of a bigger purpose. Character strengths are the most important aspect of ourselves that we want recognized and understood by others and that are important for us to express.

Let's start by looking at this issue of uniqueness. All living things— people included—have innate tendencies that define our uniqueness. Though we certainly share many commonalities, our uniqueness is what defines us as individuals. Our uniqueness speaks to our character and to what we treasure about ourselves. Unfortunately, too often we view people as lumps of clay to be molded to certain specifications or job descriptions that suit our desires, but ignore their unique needs in the process. While inanimate objects can be molded however we want, we cannot do the same to living organisms without doing harm to them.

If you see a butterfly struggling to break free of its cocoon, your instinct may be to "help" the creature along in its process. But by doing so, you destroy the emerging butterfly's ability to strengthen its wings and become what it's intended to be: a glorious, winged beauty that helps pollinate flowers. In fact, the butterfly will die due to your interference. Controlling people tend to think that they know best in every situation, but truly wise leaders create the conditions for people to flourish and soar.

What Are Character Strengths?

In a nutshell, character strengths are those aspects of your personality that define what's best in you, and they are collectively responsible for your greatest achievements and fulfillment. Scientists have identified twenty-four of them that are the basic building blocks that define our individuality as people, psychologically speaking. We each possess all twenty-four of these strengths in varying degrees and combinations.[2]

These character strengths are universally valued—in both the East and the West, and in both developed and undeveloped countries. Positive psychologists define them as positive traits that are beneficial to self and others. They lead us to positive feelings, relationships, achievements, and into engaging and meaningful life activities. We flourish once we identify and flex our strengths.[3]

Each of us expresses these strengths in varying degrees. That leads us to the next feature of the VIA character strengths: If we want to build up one or more of these strengths, we can learn to do so. You aren't born missing key character strengths; instead, you just might not have focused on exercising that particular strength, perhaps causing it to atrophy.

Dr. Seligman, one of the most eminent social scientists of our time, created and led this effort to identify what's best about human beings and how we can better use character strengths to build our best lives. He enlisted the involvement of more than fifty elite scholars who spent three years studying strengths while supported with more than one million dollars in funding. Drawing upon writings in the fields of philosophy, religion, theology, the humanities and more, they distilled the best of what we know into the VIA Classification of Character Strengths and Virtues—a feat that was lauded by renowned Harvard psychologist Howard Gardner as "the most important development in the field of psychology in the past half century."[4] Then Seligman and associates developed a scientific way of measuring these character strengths in individuals, which resulted in the VIA Survey. Millions of people worldwide have now taken this survey to discover what's best and noble about themselves. As Harvard psychologist Dr. Kauffman puts it, "As a coach I have found the VIA strengths survey to be quietly radical. Many clients have never had their strengths assessed and find that just reading the survey results helps them label or understand themselves in new ways."[5]

It's Not "Good vs. Bad"

Traditionally, character has been thought of in moralistic terms as opposed to practical terms, resulting in a black or white judgment as to whether a person is good or bad. This traditional approach leads to programs that prescribe a handful of character strengths for the way we all "should" be. Alternatively, the VIA approach recognizes that human goodness can be expressed in many ways and allows each person greater latitude to find his own way of living a "good life." Like facial characteristics, our character strengths come together in ways that define our uniqueness. So, while traditional approaches lead to efforts to make us all the same, the VIA approach leads us to embrace our uniqueness. Sizing up a person's character is no less complex a task than sizing up his physical attributes. A fair description of both ends up being a description of a variety of features.

Elevate Talent

Talent is defined as what a person can do well, and character strengths can be defined as what a person *cares* to do, which elevates that talent. One of the most important points of the VIA approach is to distinguish between talent and character strengths. While talent is important, what raises you to a higher level is connecting talent with your character strengths—who you are at your core. So, a person may have innate musical ability but never develops any talent/skills related to that ability. Or, one may develop talent/skills through music lessons and practice, but then is faced with how to direct the talent/skills: "What kind of music do I want to play?" "What music speaks to me?"

Consider a concert pianist who has innate talent. Although he has developed that talent, his musical genius is elevated by connecting his talents/skills with his character strengths: who he is as a person, what type of music he loves to play and what gets his creative juices flowing. Because of this he hears, experiences, and feels music on an elevated level. His character strengths are what make him more fully engaged and alive in his playing. The freedom to express talent in each person's unique way is what gives the world some of the greatest art, music, science, etc.

In coaching, one of my main goals is to elevate talent in my clients, so that they can experience deep satisfaction and engagement like this concert pianist. The world is littered with adults whose parents insisted on music lessons, but who never were encouraged to find the kind of music they could connect with, and who therefore completely stopped playing music as soon as they grew beyond their parents' control. It is when both talent and character strengths come together that a person is fully engaged. As Dr. Neal H. Mayerson, founder of the VIA Institute, describes it: "Character strengths are the wings upon which our talents soar."

Signature Strengths

The VIA survey report shows how strongly each of the twenty-four character strengths are represented in you. All twenty-four are important, and all are tools at your disposal. Character strengths listed toward the bottom of your report are not considered weaknesses—they are simply the ones you use less frequently.

Let's take a look at the different categories of character strengths. First, some strengths are more strongly represented in us (and therefore rise to the top of the report), and are core to our identity, to who we are. These are called our signature strengths. Like a fingerprint, our signature strengths define our uniqueness—they represent our authentic selves. Our signature strengths are those that feel almost as important to us as breathing. They come naturally, and we feel energized and satisfied when we are expressing them. And when others see them in us, we feel understood in an important way. If we are unable to express these parts of ourselves for some reason, we might feel like we are suffocating or dying inside. That's why focusing on our signature strengths and how to put them into play—at work, and in life in general—is so important.

Sometimes, listed among our middle or lesser strengths, we also find strengths that once were signature—core to our identity and expressed often. But due to neglect or discouragement from others, they are now expressed only infrequently. In my coaching work I help people reactivate these "lost signature strengths." This reclamation process can powerfully rekindle passion and purpose in a person who feels as though his or her flame has been extinguished.

Optimal Use: Avoiding Extremes

When I was asked to coach Jeff, VP of Sales for a manufacturing company, I had serious reservations about taking the job. The president of the company, Ryan, had called me as a last ditch effort to save his high-producing VP of Sales from being fired. You see, several employees in various departments within the company had filed formal complaints against Jeff because of what they called his "manipulating, demoralizing, critical, fear-based leadership style that sometimes resorted to threats." They wanted Jeff fired, but Ryan needed a high producing VP of Sales, and Jeff consistently got great sales results. I agreed to one meeting with Jeff to assess whether coaching might be of value.

The first thing we did was have Jeff take the VIA Survey of Character Strengths, because I wanted to approach the issue from a positive vantage point. I was quite frankly surprised to see that "Love" was Jeff's top strength! I wasn't so surprised to see "Bravery" close behind, and to see "Prudence" and "Teamwork" and "Social Intelligence" far down the list. When I asked Jeff about his top strength, "Love," and how he saw it manifested in his work, his reply was that he truly "loved" the company he had helped build and that he often felt protective and a strong sense of stewardship over the future of the company. He explained that it really irritated him when he encountered mistakes, and he was quite brave about telling people when they had done something wrong. I could quickly see how Jeff was "overusing" his love for the company he helped build, as well as his bravery in communicating with people. In addition, he was underusing the strengths of teamwork and prudence by neglecting relational and team-building opportunities, and by not considering how his off-the-cuff, critical comments might be interpreted by people on his team. It was as though he was determined to build a company without recognizing that unhappy, insulted coworkers would not enable his goal.

Jeff first worked on extending his love for the company to an awareness that an extension of that warmth and appreciation would best be focused on the very people he had offended. He then worked diligently on building his lesser strengths of prudence by thinking before

> When we underuse or overuse our strengths, it is often due to a loss of awareness and/or perspective.

talking, and teamwork by encouraging everyone's participation and extending respect to all. He asked for candid feedback on how he could improve, and he reported back regularly to the very people who gave him feedback, sharing his progress in the areas where they had assessed him low. It didn't get better overnight. He had to behave consistently in this new way for several months in order to rebuild trust in the damaged relationships. Six months later, Jeff again asked for feedback from coworkers. This time, all his feedback was positive. People were truly surprised by the effort he had made, and after several months came to believe that it was sincere. Jeff not only saved his job, but he was promoted and was offered equity in the company.

When we underuse or overuse our strengths, it is often due to loss of awareness and/or perspective. An example of loss of awareness might be a person who is kind and compassionate with friends, but who discovers through feedback that he does not extend this strength much in work relationships. Until he received the feedback, he was unaware that he was underusing this strength at work.

At the other end of the continuum, we can overuse our signature strengths due to a loss of perspective.[6] Our signature strengths are the strengths that we most readily express—our first "go to" strengths. Sometimes we fail to assess if there is an appropriate need for the strength. As one proverb warns, "One who is good with a hammer comes to think everything is a nail." Overuse can get us into trouble in relationships. For example, a person high in prudence can overuse that strength at work to such a degree that others perceive her as a naysayer—a person who too often discourages trying new things. Or, a creative person may fail to realize that a creative work task has moved past the point of integrating new ideas and now needs to be implemented. Or, a person who loves learning may go on *ad nauseam* about intricate details in a work process, causing his team to check out mentally. Our signature strengths can have such force of expression that we can overuse them—either in the wrong situations or at too high of an intensity.[7]

In my coaching I have found this to be one of the most powerful learning insights for people—learning to use their signature strengths well and to modulate them according to any given situation. I work with my clients to cultivate a greater awareness of how to use their character strengths optimally, and it has led to significant breakthroughs. Illustration 1 in the Appendix is a sample character strengths ranking graph to give you a visual of what your graph might look like following a survey of your character strengths.

In developing character strengths, I encourage people to aim for the "blissful middle" because avoiding extremes of underuse and overuse leads to optimal expression of strengths. Sometimes people overuse or underuse strengths and overlook using other strengths in certain situations or with certain people, all of which can cause discord in relationships.

Besides the danger of overuse, our top character strengths can also be areas of vulnerability that may leave a door open to becoming upset with others. Because we care so much about our top strengths, we tend to expect others to care as much as we do and can become upset when they do not. Take, for example, a person high in fairness who will tend to become greatly upset whenever she sees instances of others (or herself) being treated unfairly. In other words, our top strengths are also our hot buttons—that emotional trigger that fires when others act in contradiction.

Underuse occurs when we either don't use a character strength at the right level of expression or we neglect to use it in situations where it would be appropriate. Overuse can occur when we use a top strength in almost every situation without regard to its appropriateness to the situation. What we are striving for is to find the point of optimal expression between overuse and underuse. The goal is to find the right "balance."[8] You will find a helpful graphic detailing overuse and underuse as well as optimal use of strengths below.

Underuse	Optimal Use	Overuse
Conformity	Creativity	Eccentricity
Disinterest	Curiosity	Nosiness
Unreflectiveness	Judgment/Open-mindedness	Narrow-mindedness/Cynicism
Complacency	Love of Learning	Know-it-all
Shallowness	Perspective	Overbearing
Cowardice	Bravery	Foolhardiness
Fragility	Perseverance	Obsessiveness
Phoniness	Honesty	Righteousness
Sedentary	Zest	Hyperactive
Emotional Isolation	Love	Emotional Promiscuity
Indifference	Kindness	Intrusiveness
Obtuse/Clueless	Social Intelligence	Over-analyzing
Selfishness	Teamwork	Dependent
Partisanship	Fairness	Detachment
Compliant	Leadership	Authoritarian
Merciless	Forgiveness	Permissive
Baseless self-esteem	Humility	Self-deprecation
Sensation-seeking	Prudence	Stuffiness
Self-indulgence	Self-Regulation	Inhibition
Oblivion	Appreciation of Excellence	Snobbery/Perfectionism
Rugged individualism	Gratitude	Ingratiation
Negative	Hope	Pollyanna-ism
Overly serious	Humor	Giddiness
Uncertainty	Spirituality	Fanaticism

Golden Mean, (©VIA Institute on Character Golden Mean Model, All rights reserved. Used with permission.)

Situational Strengths

Situational strengths are those we can call forth in good measure when necessary. Dogs aren't known for their tree climbing abilities, but when I teach VIA workshops I show a picture of a real dog who made it halfway up a tree after a cat! The dog is calling forth a lesser strength when needed. Situational strengths are not as important in defining who we are. For example, while some people may have perseverance as a signature strength—meaning that in general they like to work at things diligently—others who do not have this as a signature strength may still be able to use their willpower to persevere when work projects require. For the first group of people, persevering marks what they love to do and is a strength that is energizing to them; but for the second group, that strength is something they call forth only when they need to perform in a given situation. Interestingly, in that situation it can be more draining. The difference between situational strengths and signature strengths is that people *need to express* signature strengths to feel whole but are comfortable expressing situational strengths *only when they are needed.*

Strengths Combinations

Character strengths—they rarely exist alone—mostly occur in combinations. Like metal alloys (*i.e.,* when iron and carbon combine to make steel), the right combinations can amplify the strengths, make them function better, and even complement each other. Take, for example, humor and social intelligence. Humor applied with too little social intelligence can be offensive (*i.e.,* telling a joke about the deceased at the funeral). Yet, when humor and social intelligence exist together, that combination becomes endearing and one of the most powerful strengths in social situations, helping to create strong relationships. Other examples of powerful strength combinations are prudence and creativity, as well as judgment and zest, because they moderate and balance each other. Sometimes, our middle strengths play the role of moderating our top strengths to make them work better. Our top strengths can combine in unexpected and extremely powerful ways.

In my twenty plus years of coaching, I have yet to encounter a more powerful tool in developing self-awareness than understanding character strengths. I have witnessed dramatic improvements in personal and interpersonal success when people set goals that are authentic and honor their core strengths while understanding and honoring the strengths in others.

Following is a list of the 24 Character Strengths organized according to the 6 Virtue Categories.

The VIA Classification of Character Strengths
6 Virtue Categories Containing the 24 Character Strengths

1. **Wisdom and Knowledge** – Cognitive strengths that entail the acquisition and use of knowledge

   - *Creativity* [originality, ingenuity]: Thinking of novel and productive ways to conceptualize and do things
   - *Curiosity* [interest, novelty-seeking, openness to experience]: Taking an interest in ongoing experience for its own sake; finding subjects and topics fascinating; exploring/discovering
   - *Judgment and Open-Mindedness* [critical thinking]: Thinking things through and examining them from all sides; not jumping to conclusions; being able to change one's mind in light of evidence; weighing all evidence fairly
   - *Love of Learning*: Mastering new skills, topics, and bodies of knowledge, whether on one's own or formally; obviously related to the strength of curiosity but goes beyond it to describe the tendency to add systematically to what one knows
   - *Perspective* [wisdom]: Being able to provide wise counsel to others; having ways of looking at the world that make sense to oneself and to other people

2. **Courage** – Emotional strengths that involve the exercise of will to accomplish goals in the face of opposition, external or internal

   - *Bravery* [valor]: Not shrinking from threat, challenge, difficulty, or pain; speaking up for what is right even if there is opposition; acting on convictions even if unpopular; includes physical bravery but is not limited to it
   - *Perseverance* [persistence, industriousness]: Finishing what one starts; persisting in a course of action in spite of obstacles; "getting it out the door"; taking pleasure in completing tasks
   - *Honesty* [authenticity, integrity]: Speaking the truth but more broadly presenting oneself in a genuine way and acting in a sincere way; being without pretense; taking responsibility for one's feelings and actions
   - *Zest* [vitality, enthusiasm, vigor, energy]: Approaching life with excitement and energy; not doing things halfway or halfheartedly; living life as an adventure; feeling alive and activated

3. Humanity – Interpersonal strengths that involve tending and befriending others

- *Capacity to Love and Be Loved*: Valuing close relations with others, in particular those in which sharing and caring are reciprocated; being close to people
- *Kindness* [generosity, nurturance, care, compassion, altruistic love, "niceness"]: Doing favors and good deeds for others; helping them; taking care of them
- *Social Intelligence* [emotional intelligence, personal intelligence]: Being aware of the motives and feelings of other people and oneself; knowing what to do to fit into different social situations; knowing what makes other people tick

4. Justice – Civic strengths that underlie healthy community life

- *Teamwork* [citizenship, social responsibility, loyalty]: Working well as a member of a group or team; being loyal to the group; doing one's share
- *Fairness*: Treating all people the same according to notions of fairness and justice; not letting personal feelings bias decisions about others; giving everyone a fair chance
  Leadership: Encouraging a group of which one is a member to get things done and at the time maintain good relations within the group; organizing group activities and seeing that they happen

5. Temperance – Strengths that protect against excess

- *Forgiveness and Mercy:* Forgiving those who have done wrong; accepting the shortcomings of others; giving people a second chance; not being vengeful
- *Modesty and Humility:* Letting one's accomplishments speak for themselves; not regarding oneself as more special than one is
- *Prudence:* Being careful about one's choices; not taking undue risks; not saying or doing things that might later be regretted
- *Self-Regulation* [self-control]: Regulating what one feels and does; being disciplined; controlling one's appetites and emotions

6. Transcendence – Strengths that forge connections to the larger universe and provide meaning

- *Appreciation of Beauty and Excellence* [awe, wonder]: Noticing and appreciating beauty, excellence, and/or skilled performance in various domains of life, from nature to art to mathematics to science to everyday experience
- *Gratitude:* Being aware of and thankful for the good things that happen; taking time to express thanks
- *Hope* [optimism, future-mindedness, future orientation]: Expecting the best in the future and working to achieve it; believing that a good future is something that can be brought about
- *Humor* [playfulness]: Liking to laugh and tease; bringing smiles to other people; seeing the light side; making/telling jokes
- *Spirituality* [faith, purpose]: Having coherent beliefs about the higher purpose and meaning of the universe; knowing where one fits within the larger scheme; having beliefs about the meaning of life that shape conduct and provide comfort

VIA Classification of Character Strengths (© VIA Institute on Character, All rights reserved. Used with permission.)

Life Sketch and the Slingshot Effect

After my coaching clients take the VIA Survey, one of the first things I do is ask them to create a "Life Sketch" that which visually depicts the peaks and valleys in a person's life. It illustrates times in life when a person felt she or he was thriving (expressing strengths) or withering (suppressing strengths). Although the valleys most often depict times of withering, occasionally a valley can represent a life challenge that has ignited significant strengths expression. An example of this is my friend Ally's battle with cancer. She feels the "valley" experience of the cancer has brought out previously underutilized strengths, and those newfound strengths have been a source of great fulfillment to her ever since. I call this the "slingshot effect." Like a slingshot, we sometimes find ourselves "pulled back" and withering intensely due to an extreme challenge. Then we reignite a forgotten or untapped strength that propels our growth further beyond our expectations.

The Life Sketch gives people an opportunity to revisit the life stories they have been telling themselves for years, look at their life experiences through the lens of character strengths, and reframe experiences in ways that better serve them going forward.

Research shows that stories are a powerful catalyst for personal growth.[9] A person's own life history can yield powerful lessons and lead to helpful insights.[10]

Below is a life sketch created by one of my coaching clients:

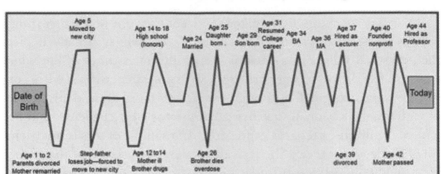

Life Sketch: Strengths Expression/Suppression, © Authentic Strengths Advantage Coaching, 2014 (Adapted from Columbia University Coaching Certification Program Life Map, Zeus and Skiffington (2003) The Coaching at Work Toolkit; Tichy's (2002) The Cycle of Leadership: How Great Leaders Teach Their Companies to Win.

Tiffany, the client who shares her life sketch above, sent me the following email about the power of reframing her life stories in ways that better serve her in the present:

> I recently was asked to participate in a focus group to assist in the creation of a support class for people who are in the midst of divorce. I was asked because I had been through a divorce, and I went as a favor to a friend. An interesting thing happened when I arrived. The participants were swapping divorce stories—who left whom, how old the kids were, how old the 'new' spouse/partner is, the financial toll incurred, the emotional fallout, etc. As I listened, I was surprised that I felt like an outsider. I wasn't sure how to tell my story (if I was asked) because my story didn't feel like part of my identity anymore. I couldn't share feelings of injustice or righteous indignation. I couldn't tell the story from a wounded place because I wasn't wounded anymore.

To be fair, I could have been right at the center of that conversation even just a year ago. I've told my story with as much drama as anyone and, in reality, it ranks up there with the best of them in terms of having been 'wronged.' But in that moment, listening to those stories, I realized how differently I see it now. I've mentally reframed it in such a way that it doesn't define me anymore. It's just part of my life journey—a left turn in the road when I thought I would be turning right. Turns out that turning left led to some amazing experiences. Turning left helped me use strengths I didn't even know I had.

For years while teaching at the university, when I introduced myself to my classes at the start of each semester, my first words were 'I'm Tiffany. I'm divorced. I'm a single mom...' These days, I start with 'I'm Tiffany. I'm a mom. I have two amazing kids...' My divorce is no longer who I am. And when I look back at it in the rearview mirror, I don't see disaster, but rather a well-worn road full of life experiences that have helped shape who I am today.

Using a worksheet to create a personal Life Sketch has multiple benefits. First of all, we can determine where we are expressing or suppressing strengths by examining life experiences. We can also see patterns that have enabled prior successes and consider how to recreate those conditions to repeat the successes. It's also possible to find potential strengths overuse, collisions, or hot buttons. In addition, identifying life themes and transitions will often trigger motivation for coaching. Creating such a sketch adds clarity to a life that might otherwise seem "scattered."

You can utilize the Life Sketch STRONG Questions© to help yourself or others more effectively identify character strengths.

STRONG Questions©: Life Sketch

- What patterns do I notice across the various stages on my Life Sketch?

- What values do I see reflected in the significant events? Strengths expression or suppression, strengths appreciation or disregard?

- What are the key messages/insights in my Life Sketch?

- What are the implications for me as I proceed with coaching?

Exercise: Best Self

Ask yourself (or the person you are coaching) to recall a time when you were energized and engaged in a project that contributed to a success. Pay attention to the character strengths that surface in the story that achieved the success. Try to see elements of the experience that could be re-created to improve a current situation or to achieve another success.

Life stories can be reframed in such a way that they offer a better, more satisfying understanding of self and can help us proceed more positively into the future as we move from "what's wrong" to "what's strong" on the path toward identifying and utilizing authentic strengths.

Coaching Tip

Make the shift from focusing on "what's wrong" to "what's strong." Take the free VIA Survey: www.viacharacter.org and encourage those you coach to take it as well. Take the time to develop the self-awareness you need to better understand and leverage your strengths personally and professionally.

STRONG Questions©: Strengths Awareness

- Do my signature strengths reflect the real, authentic me?
- Do I use my signature strengths frequently and broadly in my life–at home, at work, and/or in my community life?
- Would my family/friends be quick to identify my signature strengths?
- Do I feel more energized when I'm using my signature strengths?
- Would I feel empty inside if I were unable to express my signature strengths for a long period of time?
- What feedback have I noticed when I overuse a signature strength?
- When do my signature strengths typically become a hot button for me?
- What feedback have I noticed when I underuse a signature strength?
- How do I feel when I express a signature strength in the optimal range?
- What strengths do I typically combine to increase my effectiveness?
- What strengths have I used in my past successes?
- What strengths have I used to manage a crisis or stressor?

One of the most effective tools
we can use to increase our
OPTIMISM
is to focus on and
leverage our
strengths.

Fatima Doman

3 | THE NEUROSCIENCE OF OPTIMISM

*"Life inflicts the same setbacks and tragedies on the optimist as
on the pessimist, but the optimist weathers them better."*

—Dr. Martin E. P. Seligman

I became interested in what makes people happy precisely because I grew up in circumstances where positivity was in short supply. I was born in Angola to Portuguese parents, and my family migrated to the United States as refugees fleeing a violent revolution when I was three years old. Before we fled the country, our family survived a night where forty families in our area of the country were massacred under the cover of darkness. Terrorists had gone from farmhouse to farmhouse killing entire families with machetes.

When morning came and news spread, our little farm community congregated at a local church. Families brought mattresses and provisions and everyone huddled together for protection. Men with guns drawn watched for the next attack. Women tried to keep children quiet and calm for three days until the immediate threat had passed. My mother describes the scene that I was too young to remember clearly. The image, however, is not hard to conjure in my mind, having heard my parents tell the story many times and having felt their strong emotions as they told it. I feel transported back to that place and time. I can literally feel their fear, desperation and stress.

My parents lost everything they had worked for—their home and business—virtually overnight. Soon they found themselves in a new country, unable to speak the language, and working long and exhausting hours at manual labor. My father, an adventurous man in his youth, felt "cheated" by "bad luck" and often ruminated about what he had lost. High blood pressure and a heart condition eventually took his life too early.

My mother, a deeply religions woman, although affected by the stress, did her best to focus on the positive. Eventually, however, she began to suffer from depression and other serious health problems. Despite her challenges, my mother was often a beacon of light for me, a woman of great faith and courage. She was the fragile thread that held our family together during those tumultuous times. Although her strength waivered in the midst of such intense stress, I often heard my mother say, "Aren't we lucky to have come to the U.S.?" "We're so blessed to have survived, our entire family intact." My mother, a mild and shy 4'11" woman, had been a school teacher in Angola. However, because of the language barrier in America, she found herself working in a turkey plant on a cold, wet assembly line, cutting the breast off the bone of turkey after turkey.

She would come home, visibly tired, wearing her rubber boots and hard hat with feathers sticking to her clothes. She was scarcely through the door before she would ask about our schoolwork. She encouraged us to do our best in school, knowing that was our hope for a better life. She would come to pick me up from junior high school in her old green Ford Maverick, get out of the car wearing her hairnet and boots, and yell, "Fatinha! Estou aqui!" (Little Fatima! I'm over here!) As an awkward adolescent I sometimes felt embarrassed, wishing she would wait in the car; but today I remember those times with deep emotion and pride—my hard-working mother doing her best to raise five kids and put food on the table.

My parents were good, decent, hard-working people stretched to their limits by uncommon challenges. I grew up knowing that I wanted a different life for myself. I spent my young adult years discovering how to create a joyful life, primarily through my educational, work and spiritual development. Having been raised in a traditional Portuguese home where English was not spoken, I noticed the fingerprint of euphemisms and sayings that my parents would use on a regular basis. Sayings like "Aye Que Miseria" ("Oh, what misery!") were common to my ears.

I often longed to hear more optimistic language from my parents. At a relatively young age, I found myself wondering why some people were able to have a positive outlook on life despite hardships while others in the same situations seemed crushed by circumstances beyond their control.

It seemed as if the people who got along more easily were thinking more good thoughts and expressing more appreciation for the little things in life, developing confidence in themselves and others. I decided to be one of those people and became determined to live as if it were possible for me to have not just a good life, but to flourish. For instance, I didn't really know how I would pay for an advanced education, so I got a job as a secretary at the university in my California city where one of the benefits was taking courses, which enabled me to earn two degrees.

I began to live as if I could have a different life than the circumstances I'd been born into. My desire to explore fully how people can flourish no matter their circumstance led me to invest twenty years teaching and coaching Dr. Stephen Covey's *7 Habits of Highly Effective People*, which took me around the world, working on every continent but Antarctica. I expanded my coaching to include the transformational ideas of some of the world's most influential positive thinkers such as Martin Seligman, Stephen M.R. Covey, Barbara Fredrickson and Daniel Goleman. This insatiable appetite to understand what enables people to thrive propelled me to complete the Columbia University Coaching Certification Program where I came to understand transformational coaching techniques that changed the game for my clients as well as myself and inspired me to found my own coaching company.

I discovered that regardless of the culture, socio-economic status, and religious orientation, positive principles resonated with virtually everyone I taught around the globe. If I was teaching in Asia, people would comment on how the principles seemed to come right out of Buddhist or Taoist beliefs; when I was in Africa, I was often told that the material must have been inspired from the Koran; when working with Hindu expats, I heard that what I was teaching sounded like it came from the Bhagavad Gita, and so on. I came to realize that people were hungry for a practical way to apply their deeply valued character strengths—regardless of the origin of those strengths.

Living and working among people who strive to focus on the positive creates a remarkable foundation for supporting dreams and goals. Changing my way of thinking was like moving from living in black and white to living in color. Just as faith is the antidote to fear, optimism is the solution to bad times. When you flip the switch in your thinking, your brain gets the message and sends out new signals.

> When you flip the switch in your thinking, your brain get the message and sends out new signals.

It was a liberating shift for me. I had come to see the world through an empowering, optimistic new lens. This change greatly influenced my actions, and my new actions got me new and better results. It's the same with every person I have ever coached: the key to transformational change lies in their ability to see with new eyes, to experience a shift in perception that better serves them in their quest to improve the quality of their lives and the lives of those around them.

Positive Brain Waves

Richard Davidson, a neuroscience professor at the University of Wisconsin-Madison, has proven that monks who meditate on loving-kindness and compassion emit more powerful brain waves and generate more activity in the part of the brain that is responsible for positive emotions. "The brain is an organ built to change in response to experience," notes Davidson, Director of the Laboratory for Affective Neuroscience. "We can change our brains by changing our minds."[1]

The monks' sustained training in redirecting their thoughts and clearing their brains of negative emotions promoted an alpha-wave state of well-being. In other words, we can modify ordinary human suffering by learning to change our responses to experiences. He also points out that studies based on tens of thousands of responses to surveys demonstrate that relationships, like marriage, only provide a happiness "bump." Similarly, money does not guarantee happiness after basic needs are met. Rather, we are learning that happiness is activated by positive thoughts, a sense of purpose, balanced emotions, and a connection to something larger than self.

Dr. Martin Seligman is credited with having scientifically proven that unexpected negative events can lead to learned helplessness that puts a long-term pessimistic spin on life because of habitual expectations of adversity and powerlessness. More importantly, however, his research has shown that pessimists can be taught the skills of optimism![2] And one of the most effective tools we can use to increase our optimism is to focus on and leverage our strengths.[3]

Our Thoughts

How important are our thoughts in determining the course of our lives? Nearly 300 scientific research studies collectively conducted on more than 275,000 people internationally show that when we are in a negative state of mind, when feelings of fear, anger and discouragement are induced, our ability to solve problems decreases significantly. We literally take in less information, see fewer options to solving problems, remember less, have less patience and are more irritable, thereby straining relationships and decreasing our ability to positively influence the situation.

In sharp contrast, when study subjects focused on the positive by reading edifying literature or being shown uplifting movies, their feelings of faith, hope, and optimism grew. In turn, they consistently and significantly outperformed their study counterparts who had been exposed to negativity. Regardless of whether success was measured as a satisfying committed relationship, better health or a larger income, positive focus and outlook mattered. This result emerged consistently over time.

Positive psychology researcher Barbara Fredrickson has called this the "Broaden and Build" effect, concluding that when people focus on the positive they see more connections in puzzles—more solutions. They take in and recall more information and are more pleasant to be around and to work with, thereby strengthening their relationships and their network. In essence, our problem-solving ability and intelligence literally increase after immersion in positive and enriching influences.

Thoughts Affect Every Cell in Our Bodies

The World Health Organization has predicted that depression will be the number two leading cause of death by 2020. Widely reported as a health epidemic for more than twenty-five years, stress—often a component of depression—has continued to increase, with work providing the main environment for stress among American adults.[4]

Every thought sends an electrical signal to the brain. Thoughts affect every cell in our bodies and science is discovering that thoughts can either help or hurt our deep limbic system. Left unchecked to fester in unhealthy rumination, negative thoughts can cause havoc in your whole bodily system. Recent studies suggest that lack of positivity may be more damaging to your health than smoking, excessive drinking, or obesity. Studies reveal that people who develop more caring connections with others catch fewer colds, have lower blood pressure and are at lower risk for heart disease, Alzheimer's disease, stroke, and some cancers.[5]

Martin Seligman shared his latest research findings on how our language affects well-being at the 2013 International Positive Psychology Association conference.[6] The researchers reviewed language used in tweets by categorizing 45,000 words in the English language into positive (i.e. great, grateful, interesting, discovered, fabulous) and negative (i.e. stupid, hate, various obscenities) tweets. Over 80 million tweets in 1,200 counties in the eastern United States were included in the study. More heart attacks occurred in the counties where more negative words were tweeted. In addition, some studies have shown that, when we "harden our hearts emotionally," they harden physically as well. Research on heart patients has shown that when they experience negative emotions, the chambers of their hearts stiffen and contract.[7] Being a pessimist can, apparently, kill you, or at least make you ill.

The Power of STRONG Thoughts©

"Try to pose for yourself this task: not to think of a polar bear, and you will see that the cursed thing will come to mind every minute."

—*Fyodor Dostoevsky*

We looked at the debilitating nature of negative thoughts in chapter one. Learning how to quickly redirect negative thoughts in a positive way, rather than suppressing them, is one of the most effective ways to feel and perform better quickly. Research has also shown that peoples' attempts to suppress thoughts can actually result in a preoccupation with the very thoughts they are trying to suppress, a phenomenon researchers referred to as a rebound effect.[8] In this experiment they were told not to think about a "white bear." They were instructed to ring a bell each time they said or thought "white bear." Interestingly, when compared to a group that was told to think about white bears, the group that was asked to suppress white bear thoughts actually had significantly more thoughts on this topic. The researchers concluded that attempts at thought suppression had a paradoxical effect, suggesting that suppression might actually produce the very thought it is intended to stifle. Subsequent research has supported this notion and confirms repeated failure by people to successfully suppress unwanted thoughts.[9] So when you think, "I'm so stupid" vs. "I'm going to stop calling myself stupid," your brain really doesn't know the difference between the two thoughts and simply grabs hold of the word "stupid." What if you replaced the thought "I'm so stupid" with "Actually, I am a reflection of my top character strengths. I am creative, a leader, socially intelligent, curious, and brave. Today I will focus on these strengths and build them to feel better." I suggest creating a mantra or phrase of your character strengths to use when negative thoughts arise. One of my coaching clients, while battling cancer, would recite a mantra every time she hiked as a way to dispel the negative, fearful, ruminating thoughts about the cancer. She would say to herself, "I am brave, perseverant and hopeful. I see beauty all around me." A key to getting rid of a negative thought is replacing it with something positive, such as focusing on your strengths. The following is a three-step process I use with my clients to help them transform negative thoughts. This "STRONG Thoughts© Tool is outlined below.

The STRONG Thoughts© Tool

Step 1: Observe	Observe how negativity makes you feel. "I'm so stupid! I can't believe I dropped the ball on that project! I'm a failure." Negative thoughts cause stress chemicals to be released in your body, e.g., muscle tension, faster heart rate, shallow breathing, sweating, dizziness, lack of awareness, foggy thinking. Contrast this with how differently positive thoughts affect your body—e.g., relaxed muscles, decreased heart rate, deeper breathing, energized, aware and focused.
Step 2: Replace	Replace negative thoughts quickly with objective language that utilizes your strengths best suited to the situation. In other words, observe the situation as if you were coaching yourself and reminding yourself of all the ways your character strengths can help you better deal with or solve the issue. For example, "I am learning from this experience. I am calling forth my strengths of love and learning, social intelligence and teamwork to have a productive talk with my boss and take responsibility in a constructive way that builds our relationship and his trust in me."
Step 3: Affirm	Affirm the authentic view of yourself. Close your eyes, take a few deep breaths, and visualize yourself using the strengths you just called forth in the challenging situation. See yourself behaving in this higher, more ennobling and more productive way. Affirm these strengths in yourself until you feel differently about the situation and yourself. For example, visualize the details of the constructive conversation you will have with your boss and create in your mind the outcome you want.

STRONG Thoughts Tool, © Authentic Strengths Advantage, 2014

Where You Look Is Where You'll Go

I live in a mountain town with many advanced mountain biking trails. My friend Marissa, an avid mountain biker, shared an interesting insight with me. She noticed that the more she feared hitting a rock, the more she focused on the rocks, and the more she hit rocks! She decided one day to change her focus and look for the smooth paths instead of watching for the rocks. She found her ride was much smoother. She literally went where she looked. Marissa was on to something that world famous Olympian Noelle Pikus-Pace and many other great athletes have discovered—the power of focus and visualization.

Noelle Pikus-Pace won the silver in the skeleton event in the 2014 Winter Olympics. She lives not far from my home in Park City, Utah, and I have watched her rebound from many devastating setbacks over the years—starting with shattering her leg in a bobsledding accident—before she finally achieved her Olympic dream. Careening down an unforgiving track head first at seventy-eight miles per hour is not for the faint of heart. When she was asked what makes the most difference in a successful ride, she said, "It's what direction you are facing. You go where you look." That quote made me smile, because that simple statement is true in coaching. What we set our sights and our hearts on becomes the trajectory for our lives.

One of the most important behaviors that contributes to goal success is getting crystal clear on what you really want, and then carefully visualizing every step along the way. Once you do that, you can keep your eye on the prize, because what our hometown Olympian said is true: "You go where you look."

Visualization Is Key to High Performance

Visualization is like a mental rehearsal and has been successfully used since the Soviets made it their competitive advantage in sports in the 1970s. World-class athletes regularly invoke vivid, extremely detailed mental simulations of their athletic performance from start to finish. World champion golfer Jack Nicklaus once said, "I never hit a shot, not even in practice, without having a very sharp, in-focus picture of it in my head."

Studies on the brain are revealing that thoughts can produce similar mental processes as actions. Scientists are learning that mental imagery affects our motor control, perception, attention, planning, and memory. Therefore, real performance training occurs in the brain during visualization. We are learning that mental simulations increase motivation, confidence, and enhanced performance.[10]

STRONG Visualization© Exercise

1. **Visualize** yourself successfully using a character strength(s) best suited to a challenging situation. For example, imagine yourself in a work meeting where you are deploying your strengths of teamwork to create an atmosphere of collaboration on your team.

2. **Invoke** a clear mental picture utilizing as many of your senses as possible. Visualize your environment, including

sights, sounds and smells, who will be there, what you are wearing, etc. You can combine this visualization with self-talk, such as, "I generate teamwork and creativity with my colleagues."

3. **Practice** this visualization at least once each day. A powerful time to visualize is during exercise, upon arising in the morning or going to bed at night, or any time you are in an environment conducive to focus.

It's possible to improve what we can accomplish by creating a clear mental picture of ourselves successfully using our character strengths to handle a challenging situation.

Neuroplasticity

We can gradually develop more productive thoughts by building our strengths the same way we build a muscle. The principle of regular exercise applies here: our new strengths-focused thoughts are developed consistently, and they gradually become stronger day by day. When my clients "get real" in coaching and begin to look honestly at the link between their thoughts and behaviors, I often ask, "How is that serving you?" That one question often prompts them to consciously choose strengths-focused thoughts and behaviors that serve their vision of their best selves and lead them to live life consciously rather than by default.

Scientists are learning a great deal about our brain's ability to adapt and rewire. The old thinking was that our neurons and brain cells were limited and could not rebound after an accident or after a certain age. In the past decade, neuroscientists have discovered the brain is much more changeable than hardly anyone expected. This phenomenon, known as neuroplasticity, demonstrates that there are concrete and provable benefits to exercising the brain for more beneficial performance. What we think about can literally change our brains.

We can engage in regular practices that develop strengths in areas that have been weaknesses for us—where we usually behave in ways we later regret. Just like the athlete who works out a group of muscles over time to perform better in a sport, we can develop new neuropathways over time that will improve how we show up in our personal and professional lives—our relationships, our work, our health habits, and how well we stick to and accomplish any goal in general.

Flourishing at Any Age

Many people worry about aging and the pressure to look and remain young. Today's world of photo-shopped glamour magazines can heighten our stress levels by imposing unrealistic and disheartening expectations on people as they age. It is encouraging to see people deal with the stressors of aging with positivity, courage and connection to others. The *Journal of Personality and Psychology* published a study that demonstrated that people with positive attitudes toward aging lived longer than those plagued with negativity about getting older. Interviews with centenarians have shown that they are positive thinkers. Our attitudes and perceptions have a huge impact on our health and how we age.

My dear friend, Lucy Dettmer, first played tennis against popular television host Regis Philbin in 1993 when he heard there was a seventy-four-year-old undefeated grandmother on a college team. She won. He called for a rematch in 2006 when she was eighty-six, and she beat him again. Lucy has won thirty-six national senior tennis championships since the age of seventy-four. Her most recent two world championships were won at age ninety! I just began taking tennis lessons from Lucy, and I'm worn out by the end of each session.

I asked Lucy to what she attributes her long life and vibrancy. The biggest factor, said Lucy, "Always dwell on the positive." Her philosophy is "pick the good stuff, don't mess around with the rest." Lucy intentionally builds her character strengths by seeking out positive people, inspiring literature, art, activities, and movies. Come to think of it, I don't recall ever hearing Lucy say something negative about anyone.

Lucy is adventurous and resilient. At age sixty-two, Lucy and her husband decided to ride their bikes across the U.S.—the oldest people to ever do so. It took them forty-one days coast to coast. Up until the day they set off on the trek, the farthest they had ever ridden in one outing was twenty-five miles!

She also seeks what is honest, authentic, and natural: "Some people work so hard to create a persona, and it isn't really their true self."

When Lucy lost her husband of sixty-five years, she challenged herself to transcend her aching, overwhelming sense of loneliness by getting out and helping people—"Everyone experiences loss, and you have to figure out how you handle it...You can't wait for good things to fall in your lap—you've got to go out and find the good things, you've got to go for it." And Lucy does just that. At age ninety-six, Lucy and her daughter Peggy volunteer their time knitting caps for infants in third world countries. Although she doesn't belong to a specific religion, Lucy works with a local church teaching English in the Hispanic community. Research shows people who engage in volunteer service live on average ten years longer than others who don't.[11]

When I hike with her, she often stops and takes in all the scenery— pointing out the beauty around us, the blooming sweet peas, the Indian paintbrush, the buttercups. She notices all the little, hard-to-observe, obscure beauties of nature and revels in them. I watch her closely in these moments of deep appreciation of the beauty around her, and it's as though every cell in her body drinks in the positivity. She looks so energized, alive and youthful during these times. By the way, she kicks butt hiking, and she often goes twice a day, in addition to teaching tennis lessons, clocking seven to nine miles per day on her pedometer.

What's Lucy's secret to living a vibrant life well into her nintety-sixth year? What makes her so special? Can each of us develop Lucy's character strengths of gratitude, appreciation of beauty and excellence, hope, zest, and perseverance? Lucy thinks we can. The good news about getting up in years, according to Martin Seligman, is that creativity gets better as we age. People become more generative; they want to do good things for the world, especially as they age. Collaboration, integration, leadership skills, and persuasion all grow with age. Even better, all these "strengths" are learnable and teachable, so we can "build" a more creative world at any age.

Flourishing with Strengths

Can you learn to be happier? Research suggests that balancing pleasure, which is short-term, with meaning or purpose, which is long-term, promotes happiness. Just as we may take golf lessons or violin lessons to promote mastery in sports or music, we can be coached into an emotional balance that will allow us to operate in a more fulfilling and happier state. Aristotle said that the proper realization of our potential leads to eudaimonia, which has been defined variously as "happiness" or "human flourishing." To flourish is to enable others to flourish as well, which is what the task of the coach encompasses.

I attended Barbara Fredrickson's session at the 2013 Third World Congress on Positive Psychology titled, "Flourishing and the Genome" where she described her latest findings on "hedonic" well-being (feeling good, satisfaction/interest) compared to a "eudonic" (doing good, meaning/purpose). Both hedonic and eudonic well-being are equally opposite of depression at the level of consciousness, because they feel good and pull you out of depression. But it is significant to note that they have different effects at the cellular level. When people just experience positive emotions, those emotions don't tend to affect the positive cellular response unless they are channeled into positive *purpose*—into action. As Fredrickson said, "You can coast for a while if you have positive thinking, but those thoughts don't anchor in real cellular well-being unless you engage in meaningful and purposeful action."[12]

Research at the University of California, San Francisco indicates that the following "eudonic rewards" have a positive effect on depression, anxiety, relationships, blood pressure, overspending, overworking, overeating, and addictions:

- **Sanctuary**: Feeling secure and peaceful from within

- **Authenticity**: Feeling whole, self-accepting and genuine

- **Vibrancy**: Feeling at your best, physically fit, energetic, with a zest for life

- **Integrity**: Aware of one's purpose in life, and honoring the principles that are most important to you

- **Intimacy**: Securely connected to yourself so that you do not merge with others or distance from them; able to be separate but close

- **Spirituality**: Compassion for yourself and for others[13]

As you can see, all of these eudonic rewards are directly connected to the expression of various character strengths. An ever-expanding body of knowledge on strengths empowers people to use strengths to benefit themselves and others. "The old

> **This is core and universal and will work in every culture.**

thinking used to be that if you were dissatisfied and frustrated, you'd go out and change the world, whether you enjoyed it or not," said Dr. Ed Diener, President of the International Positive Psychology Association, during an interview I conducted with him. "The new idea is that you actually function better if you're in a positive mood. Find something you enjoy that helps people and go have fun doing it."[14] His latest studies are on how using our character strengths (virtues) affects our happiness. His research is showing "this is core and universal and will work in every culture."

Positive attitudes change everything. They create more than just good feelings. They create the ability to feel and express joy, compassion, empathy, love, gratitude, awe, reverence and, yes, success. And they are the key to doing well in a variety of ways: social relationships, health, professional accomplishments, community contributions, and stable, happy families.

Live Life "As If"

Sharon wanted to go to college so badly that she decided to live with the conviction that it would happen. Her thinking was quite a departure from reality since her parents were living at a storage facility where they were caretakers. She enrolled and went through all the motions of getting prepared to leave for school—all without knowing how her tuition would be paid. A month before payment was due, she started getting letters from friends, family, and community members who were so touched by her unshakeable faith that they felt called to contribute a little bit via a "graduation gift." By the time she had to submit a check for her first semester's tuition, she had enough money for a year. She'd had no idea how she would be able to attend the school of her dreams but had complete faith that if she lived as if she were committed to the action, the means would present itself. And it did.

Star performers learn to push aside their fear. They live with the conviction that life will work better if they are optimistic. When the situation demands, they have learned how to call forth strengths such as hope, perseverance, creativity and bravery—to mention a few. When asked what was instrumental in accomplishing the seemingly impossible goal of eight gold medals at the 2008 Olympics, Michael Phelps responded that he only allowed in positive thoughts and reframed negative feedback from naysayers into fuel for his accomplishment. He taped articles to his locker about how it would be impossible for him to win eight gold medals and used them for inspiration to energize him to do something new and unthinkable. No one can say he didn't practice to get his body in shape for the challenges of the Olympics. But, equally as important, he visualized himself achieving those eight gold medals.

Make it your goal to harness the power of optimism by visualizing how you want *your* life to be!

Coaching Tip

Commit your answers to these questions to paper and revisit them. Studies show that daily noting of what makes us happy and grateful significantly boosts our level of life satisfaction. Encourage those you coach to do the same.

STRONG Questions©: Focus

- Which of my character strengths bring out optimism in me?
- Which of my character strengths help me cope with stress/adversity?
- What are my accomplishments/victories since last week? Where can I do better next time?
- What am I grateful for today, this week?
- What can I think about or visualize each morning to approach the day from a strengths lens?
- What about my positive outlook is infectious to others?
- When in the last week have I been uplifted by music, people, art, sports, nature or science? What was inspiring about it?

Neglecting one key area of our overall self throws everything else off **KILTER**

Fatima Doman

4 | COACHING THE WHOLE PERSON

"Your mind affects your body. Your mental health affects your physical health. This in turn affects your mental health again. These are not separate systems. They are intertwined and interconnected in subtle and sophisticated ways you need to understand."

—Dr. Mark Hyman, *The UltraMind Solution*

Stopping to get gas at a convenience store not long ago, I realized many of us are killing ourselves with our choices. The manager of the store, a friend of mine, was sitting on a bench outside taking a break. He was smoking and drinking a gigantic soda. In his early thirties, he weighs somewhere around 450 pounds.

Surrounded by cigarette butts on the ground, my friend looked desperately tired and sad. I knew he battled depression and had been neglecting his physical health for a long time. He had failed to pay attention to his body, his vehicle for living. He was obese, like thirty-four percent of U.S. adults aged twenty and over.[1] He was a smoker, like 26.2 million men and 20.9 million women.[2] He was at risk for diabetes (if not already diagnosed), like 29.1 million Americans,[3] as well as a host of other preventable diseases associated with smoking and obesity. His issues with depression are not uncommon, as depression has increased tenfold in the last fifty years according to Bruce E. Levine, author of *Surviving America's Depression Epidemic*.[4]

I couldn't help wondering how different his life might be, as well as the lives of those around him, if my friend's health issues had been addressed as a systemic problem. He was not simply obese, not just a smoker, nor was the answer to his physical problems that he was depressed. He was caught in a vicious cycle, one malady worsening the other.

Fighting the Depression/Anxiety Epidemic

The World Health Organization estimates that depression affects about 121 million people worldwide and is the leading cause of disability, accounting for almost twelve percent of all disability. Depression is the second leading cause of workplace disability. Both absenteeism—feeling too low to come into the office—and presenteeism—being in the office but too energy-depleted and depressed to accomplish much—take a toll on the workplace. Depression now ranks as the fastest-growing cause of death; and it is the third leading cause of death, exceeded only by heart disease and diabetes.[5]

Depression is often associated with stress, and increasingly, research is linking the connection between stress and illness. According to the World Health Organization, a shocking 18.1 percent of Americans ages eighteen and older suffer from some sort of stress or anxiety disorder.[6] That's forty million people in the United States alone. Depression, stress and anxiety disorders are a symptom of many potential causes that should be explored with a qualified health professional.

Although there are many factors that often seem insurmountable, drawing on our character strengths is one of the most powerful and motivating tools we have to create a healthier future. Granted, sustainable change requires digging deep and drawing on everything inside us; but the fact remains that we do not have to continue to make unhealthy choices by default. By engaging all four elements—mind, body, heart, and spirit—we can coach the whole person, not just haphazardly pay attention to the parts of our lives that are currently screaming out for attention. For example, the mind corresponds to skills, capabilities, critical and creative thinking, and mental focus. To function, the body has basic needs that must be met: shelter, nutrition, rest, and recovery time. The heart desires love, trust, and respect. This translates to healthy relationships, friendships, and networks. The spirit is that part of us that hungers for meaning and purpose, a cause greater than self. The healthier you are in all four of these areas, the more engaged you will be and the better you will perform.

The convenience store manager was actually in possession of a treasure: his own authentic character strengths. With time and effort, his newly discovered strengths would motivate a healthy shift in his behaviors that would recharge his mind, body, heart, and spirit.

Strengths and Well-being

Paying attention to and making the most of your character strengths is associated with a number of positive health behaviors such as promoting a feeling of well-being, living an active life, pursuing enjoyable activities, healthy eating, and valuing physical fitness. While self-regulation had the highest associations overall in a recent study, the strengths of curiosity, appreciation of beauty, excellence, gratitude, hope, humor, and zest also displayed strong connections with health behaviors.[7]

Furthermore, character strengths have been highly correlated with well-being subscales of self-acceptance and purpose, as well as good physical and mental health.[8] In yet another study, the people who make strong use of their strengths experienced greater well-being, which was related to both their physical and mental health. Strengths use was a unique predictor of subjective well-being.[9]

Energy Is Interdependent

Our energy is interdependent just as our global economy has proven to be. Neglecting one key area of our overall self throws everything else off kilter. "Connection," "interdependence," "networks," and "systems" are buzzwords of the twenty-first century.

Whether you are coaching yourself, have a personal coach, or are coaching someone else, your overall success may depend upon addressing all aspects of your being. Old school thinking was to go to a gym and workout, see your doctor for regular check-ups, and avoid red meat and your health would be fine. Similarly, organizations would provide membership in a gym, health insurance, and vegetarian entrees in the cafeteria and call it a day. But better results can be achieved now by paying attention to integrated systems.

> There is no optimum functioning without taking care of our biological needs — rest, recovery, the proper nutrition, and physical movement.

While some successful CEOs and executives work out regularly, addressing physical and mental issues at the same time by releasing stress, I have coached others who were neglecting their health completely, erroneously thinking their key to success was complete and utter devotion to their companies or organizations. Through coaching they came to see that misplacement of attention was only cutting short their own lives and negatively influencing the lives of their colleagues and families. There is no optimum functioning without taking care of our biological needs—rest, recovery, proper nutrition, and physical movement.

When physical system problems are addressed, treating root causes instead of symptoms, many psychological issues resolve themselves. Chairman of the Institute for Integrative Medicine, Mark Hyman writes, "We have all heard of the mind-body connection or how our thoughts affect the health of our body. But the reverse is far more powerful: what you do to your body, your basic biology, has a profound effect on your brain."[10]

Use Your Strengths to Recharge

You can increase your desire to recharge the mind, body, heart, and spirit by using your character strengths to energize your activities.[11] For example, if you have a signature strength of "appreciation of beauty and excellence," your body recharging activity could be hiking or running outside in the beauty of nature. If you have a signature strength of "teamwork," your mind recharging activity could be to organize a book group to discuss new insights from the book being reviewed. If you have a signature strength of leadership, your heart recharging activity could be to organize an outing to get to know more people in your neighborhood. If you have a signature strength of kindness, your spirit recharging activity could be to donate your time feeding the homeless. The more you connect your character strengths to activities that recharge you, the more likely it is that you will enjoy and continue the positive behaviors.

Recharge the Body

There is no question that the mind influences the body. Dr. Andrew Steptoe of University College London probed the biological connection between happiness and health in a study published in the American Journal of Epidemiology. The study showed that positive emotions are connected with biological responses that are "health-protective."[12] A study of 193 healthy volunteers by Carnegie Mellon University provided evidence that happiness can strengthen the immune system, according to Dr. Sheldon Cohen.[13] After exposure to cold viruses, volunteers with high levels of positive emotions were more resistant to disease. Numerous studies show that happiness can protect against becoming ill, as well as extend lifespan in healthy individuals.

Perhaps the most powerful tool you have to improve your health, however, is your fork. All calories are not equal. Food has information and talks to your genes, according to Mark Hyman, turning them on or off. "Food is the fastest-acting and most powerful medicine you can take to change your life," according to *The UltraMind Solution*.[14] Dr. Hyman's Seven Keys to UltraWellness include optimizing nutrition, balancing your hormones, cooling off inflammation, fixing your digestion, enhancing detoxification, boosting energy metabolism, and calming your mind.

Getting the amount of sleep your body needs is paramount. Set goals for your physical fitness by regularly incorporating aerobic, strength training and flexibility exercises. Include fresh vegetables, fruit and lean protein in your diet. Remember to drink approximately two and a half liters (about eight glasses) of water on a daily basis. Being dehydrated can cause fuzzy thinking, headaches, and blood circulation problems. Take a brief stretch break after every ninety-minute work session whenever possible—this will enable blood flow to your brain.

Recharge the Mind

The average person works about 11,000 days between their mid-twenties and age sixty-five. That's a long time if you're unfulfilled or disengaged at work. The brain is like a muscle—if we don't use it, it will atrophy. In fact, in a famous study of the brains of retired Catholic nuns autopsied after their deaths in their eighties and nineties, several showed lesions on the brain associated with Alzheimer's disease yet they had not exhibited symptoms of the disease. The researchers determined that their high levels of engagement with community and continuing to strive to learn new things literally saved them from the dementia associated with the disease.

At birth, your brain had about a trillion neural connections. That sounds like a lot, but remember, we're talking about a baby brain. The best way to grow more connections is to take up a challenging activity that's new to you, like computers/technology, music, or a foreign language. Flex your brain "muscle" to keep those neurons firing and making new connections. Challenges should offer novelty and fun. Strive to learn something new.

According to one study, taking piano lessons for even four months can improve young people's performance on math tests by an average of twenty-seven percent.[15] Some suggestions to renew yourself mentally might be:

- Become a reader
- Take fun courses that interest you
- Peruse the internet for topics that grow your mind
- Explore hobbies and find something that brings you joy

Recharge the Heart

Developing emotional intelligence can help us understand the source of our emotions and help us develop positive relationships with ourselves and others.

Once when I was teaching a class on strengthening relationships, a participant pulled me aside and said the biggest insight for her was learning that she didn't have to go to her spouse with every negative emotion she felt. Instead, she could work through her emotions without burdening him with her struggle to find a personal solution. She found that the key to solving her relationship problems could be taking responsibility for and better managing her emotions and adjusting her perspective so that she could present herself with a sense of clarity and optimism to those close to her.

Learn to use "I" statements such as "I feel frustrated when I spend hours working alone on a task that I understood to be a team effort," rather than "you" statements such as "You always dump the work on my shoulders, and I get no help!" Using the "I" statement demonstrates taking responsibility for one's feelings, while deploying the "you" statement places blame, eliciting defensiveness in the relationship.

Do we have unrealistic expectations of another person? Constant rehashing of negative experiences is not productive. Coaching can teach us to focus on the present, where the solution is. It's okay to briefly visit the past for context, but it is not healthy to live there. Constant rumination can be the sign of a "brain type" which can be ameliorated with targeted nutrition, environmental changes, and behavior modification, among other strategies. Many competent health professionals specialize in this area.

Take time to nurture your important personal relationships by spotting character strengths in those close to you, and make an effort to spend quality time with those you love. Improve your professional relationships by recognizing and appreciating strengths in your colleagues.

Recharge the Spirit

Giving service is an excellent way to renew ourselves spiritually, and the personal benefits we reap are an added bonus. It literally improves your health. Research shows that those who are connected to their communities and give back, experience a boost in their immune systems, their wounds heal faster and they catch colds and other infections less frequently.[16] Remember my friend Lucy who is enjoying an active, vibrant, service-oriented ninety-sixth year of life?

Other ways to renew spiritually are reading inspirational biographies, listening to uplifting music, or being inspired by nature. Studies on positivity have found that people who spent twenty minutes or more outside in decent weather experienced a boost in their moods. They also demonstrated improved memory as well as more expansive and open thinking.[17]

Entrepreneur Clay Mathile, former owner and chairman of The Iams Company and founder of Aileron, a nonprofit that fosters entrepreneurship on the principles of learning, doing and giving back to communities, literally tried to reserve Fridays for what he called "blue sky days." He found that a change of scenery and keeping his calendar open at least one day a week led him to new ideas and rejuvenation. At Aileron, he's installed a "blue sky" room for the entrepreneurs who visit the center to use for contemplation.

Virtually all studies show that people who practice some form of spiritual devotion are happier. Spirituality can involve committing to a life of integrity to our values, listening to inspirational and uplifting music, serving in our community, or practicing spiritual worship that edifies. One of the key components of spirituality is feeling positive emotions that connect you to something greater than self.

Connecting to your character strengths is a spiritual renewal in and of itself. In fact, using your strengths to recharge all four areas of your being will make the process much more enjoyable and meaningful!

The Shift from "No" to "Yes"

"Fatima, my cancer is back," said an executive I'd been coaching in Sweden. Steve, who leads a division of a company, had already had one bout with cancer and this would be his second round of chemotherapy.

He told me in our first coaching session that when he was alone in his room, he would yell at himself for not being good enough. "You're so stupid," he'd yell into the mirror.

Although he exuded confidence and ability to others, he said inside he had no confidence, in part he believed due to an overly critical father, whose voice had become his inner critic. He felt like he was playing a role and conning people into thinking he was a capable person. He worried that the façade would someday be discovered. The truth is that he was an extremely competent and talented leader. But that didn't change the fact that this accomplished man lacked confidence and was so unhappy. He had multiple failed marriages and had recently attached himself to a married woman who chose to go back to her husband.

Acknowledging a possible connection between his self-criticism and manifesting disease, he made a commitment to start using positive self-talk to silence his inner critic immediately upon noticing negative thoughts. He gradually became more relaxed and let down his constant guard. As a result, he came across as more authentic and approachable to his colleagues and friends, which in turn strengthened and inspired trust in his relationships. After making some progress toward his goals, he was offered a promotion, and the married girlfriend wanted him back, but he was now unsure. He was finally making better choices, but his cancer had returned.

Steve had met all his coaching goals in the past three months and had developed better relations with his subordinates, yet he still scored himself quite low, while everyone else scored him high. He decided to start saying "How fascinating!" as part of his self-acceptance and to discover what other people thought he was doing well—to look through their less critical lens at himself.

Steve had always found it so hard to say *no* to unhealthy relationships and requests that drained him. He called himself a "pleaser." We talked about the concept that it is easier to say *no* to what is not serving you when there is a much more meaningful *yes* lighting the way for you. He decided to start saying *yes* to what was important to him instead of what was important only to others. He said *yes* to exercise, more sleep and better nutrition. *Yes* to ending the relationship with the married woman. *Yes* to meeting an emotionally available partner and to opening a place in his heart and mind for a healthy relationship.

Saying *yes* opened up a new world for Steve. He identified healthy practices on all four levels—mind, body, heart, spirit—to say yes to. Steve had felt so heavy and overwhelmed before, but things became lighter; and it was fun to spend time and energy on the yeses. Many things began to improve for him, including his relationships and his health. He found a way to reframe the negative by saying yes and evoking what was good for him—what he wanted in his life—rather than carrying the burden of focusing on what he didn't want.

Whole Life Thriving

A 2009 Harvard Business Review report titled *What Coaches Can Do for You* (2009) shows the direct link between coaching and personal application.[19] Even when people hired coaches for purely professional reasons (which happens ninety-seven percent of the time), the coaching conversations tended to cross over into personal life matters (such as work/life balance, relationships, energy maintenance and so forth) about seventy-six percent of the time. These statistics clearly indicate that coaching is more successful when it involves the whole person.

During my twenty years of coaching people to achieve greater life balance, I have utilized many life balance and time management tools. I have synthesized what I found to be the key components of these various tools, including Co-Active Coaching's "Wheel of Life," into one tool that I now use with greater success in my strengths coaching process.[18] The Whole Life Scale© I have developed helps people look deeply at all areas of their lives and target specific ways they can create more fulfillment by cultivating not only balance, but also joyful, enriching goals that enable them to thrive.

As you will see below, the Whole Life Scale© is divided into eight columns, labeled for different areas of life, *i.e.,* work, fun, physical space, finances, mind, body, heart, and spirit. The exercise measures on a scale from zero to ten your fulfillment "snapshot" in each of the areas on the day you work through the exercise. It is not a report card. When you plot out your Whole Life Scale©, you may see some "empty space" in the scale, where you scored areas of your life lower than you would like. This empty space represents an opportunity to leverage your character strengths to create greater fulfillment in these areas of your life. The areas where you may have scored yourself as highly fulfilled are to be celebrated and used as guideposts for developing the other areas. For example, if you already know how to use your character strengths to create fulfillment in the "heart (relationships)" area of your life, perhaps you can replicate that successful process in developing the "work (engagement/career development)" area of your life.

WHOLE LIFE SCALE©

The ASA Whole Life Scale© measures fulfillment in key areas of life. Score yourself on a scale of 1-10 with 1 being the lowest level of fulfillment and 10 being the highest level of fulfillment in each area of your life. Explore ways to improve your fulfillment in the areas where you scored low. Celebrate the areas where you scored high and continue to develop those areas.

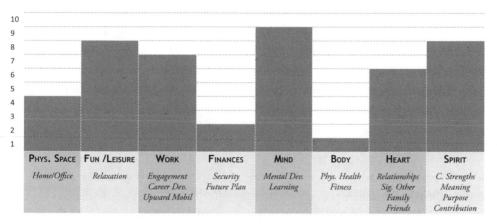

PHYS. SPACE	FUN /LEISURE	WORK	FINANCES	MIND	BODY	HEART	SPIRIT
Home/Office	Relaxation	Engagement	Security	Mental Dev.	Phys. Health	Relationships	C. Strengths
		Career Dev.	Future Plan	Learning	Fitness	Sig. Other	Meaning
		Upward Mobil				Family	Purpose
						Friends	Contribution

One of my clients, a manager at a university who had recently been promoted to an executive level, came to see me because she was intimidated by the demands of her new job. Far from celebrating her success, her promotion was so stressful that she was nearly incapacitated by her fear of failure. She spent countless overtime hours working in a cluttered, drab workspace that she called "disheartening and overwhelming." She had stopped exercising in an effort to squeeze out more time from the day, started living on fast foods from the vending machine, and gradually gained thirty pounds. She couldn't sleep soundly and was unsure how to meet all the new demands; in addition, her anxieties spilled over into her personal life. She found it impossible not to think about work while at home and on vacation—which was frustrating to her husband as well.

The first thing we did was to use the Whole Life Scale© to measure her fulfillment in all areas of her life. She was able to quickly see a visual of how most of the areas of her life were being affected—with some of the areas such as physical space, work, physical health, and fun ranking only a two in fulfillment/satisfaction. She then spent time clarifying her vision of her ideal future, which helped her identify the strengths she would call forth to produce greater life balance and fulfillment in these areas. When she was clear on what was truly important to her, she began to cultivate a whole life by better balancing all areas of her life and to achieve greater fulfillment in those areas. She now begins each day at work by listening to soft music, places fruit and healthful snacks within eyesight on her desk, takes at least one stress break during the day for a fifteen-minute walk, and has re-positioned her desk so that she no longer has her back to her office window, but instead can see the trees outside.

She regained her energy and was able to think more clearly once she could distinguish between what she called "the noise of unproductive work demands" and "the activities that empowered her ideal future." The activities that contributed to meaning, purpose and productivity were the ones she said *yes* to—things like planning and building relationships. She learned she could say "let's schedule a time" or "not until after I finish this project" for the less important busywork some people requested of her. She learned to allow her purpose and vision to guide her. She performed so well in her new job that she has now been promoted again.

It's easier not to get sidetracked if you can say *no* to things you do not believe in because you have examined what you want to say *yes* to. By focusing on what we "want" instead of what we "don't want," we can tap into the motivating, energizing deeper *yes*.

Coaching Tip

Notice which of the four key areas (mind, body, heart, spirit) you typically avoid recharging. That is likely the area in need of the most attention. For optimum performance, all areas should receive attention.

STRONG Questions©: Recharge

Recharge Mind
What strengths of the mind can I build/develop this week?
What new learning will I explore?
How will I develop an inner coach mindset this week?

Recharge Body
What healthy food choices and exercise would give me the greatest energy and vitality?
What is the amount of sleep that my body thrives on?
How will I create more active relaxation and revitalization in my life?

Recharge Heart
What strengths of the heart can I develop this week?
What is one thing I will do this week to develop my important relationships?
How will I recognize and appreciate strengths in others?

Recharge Spirit
What strengths of wisdom/transcendence can I develop this week?
What inspires, uplifts and edifies me?
How can I better serve in my most important relationships and in my community?

Part II | EMPOWER YOUR STRENGTHS

"When clients learn to bring their strengths to a challenge it helps them tap into their intrinsic motivations and can help them improve performance and find more satisfaction in the task accomplishment."

—Dr. Carol Kauffman

"After exploring strengths, it is time to move to stage two and empower those strengths with sustainable strengths motivation. We seek constructive feedback and envision how we will use that feedback to create our ideal future. Then we will have the necessary building blocks for setting and achieving STRONG Goals.©"

—Fatima Doman

ENGAGE
Strengths in Action
Reflect, Reveal, Recalibrate/CSQ

EMPOWER
Strengths Motivation
Feedback/Feed Forward
Motivation Grid/STRONG Goals

EXPLORE
Strengths Awareness
Life Sketch/Whole Life Scale
Best Self/STRONG Filter/STRONG Thoughts

CHARACTER STRENGTHS

AUTHENTICITY is a collection of choices that we have to make every day. It's about the choice to show up and be real. The choice to let our true selves be seen.

Dr. Brené Brown

5 | AUTHENTIC MOTIVATION

"The well-being that using our signature strengths engenders is anchored in authenticity. But just as well-being needs to be anchored in strengths and virtues, these in turn must be anchored in something larger. Just as the good life is something beyond the pleasant life, the meaningful life is beyond the good life."

—*Dr. Martin E.P. Seligman*

Potential

We are born with everything we need to lead fulfilling lives. All twenty-four character strengths can be found in all human beings across the globe. Some of us are born into environments that cloud our access to that inner wisdom. Yet, even in the worst of circumstances people defy odds and rise above their surroundings. Why? People from every culture attest to an innate sense of direction or conscience expressed in their strengths, an inner compass that guides them.

Rodney, while a homeless teen in the streets of Cincinnati, was shot as he was being robbed. After several surgeries he began to recover physically but had sunk into a deep depression. Through the guidance of a community service worker, Rodney ended up in a VIA workshop. He said when he read his survey results, he saw so much of himself that he wasn't connecting with and that discovering his strengths opened up a whole new world for him. He had never had anyone notice strengths in him, and he began to see possibilities for himself. In Rodney's words,

"These are things I can build on and move forward with in my life. The best part of my life is in front of me, not behind me." He now leads a community outreach program where he teaches hip-hop to encourage kids to get off the street and express themselves in a positive way. In Rodney's words, "Everybody has a gift. EVERYBODY. And your gifts can be the solution to your problems." Some of us have not yet unwrapped the gifts we were born with, and others have been born into environments that don't acknowledge our gifts; but the gifts are there nonetheless. Every human being regardless of circumstances possesses this potential.

There are scores of historic examples of people who tapped into their character strengths, who had a vision and sense of mission that guided their actions, and who seemed to have been destined to lead others on an inspired path. Gandhi and Martin Luther King, Jr., come to mind. They had visions of nonviolent resistance that led them to become role models for masses who gathered to follow them in the cause of human rights.

But how did Bono—lead singer of the band U2, which has won twenty-two Grammy awards since 1976—become a world thought leader and force for peace? Growing up in Ireland in the 1960s and 1970s as the son of a Catholic postal worker and a Protestant mother, he had a personal understanding of how religious differences can lead to war if the factions are not united in one vision for humanity. As he became more successful in his music career, he did not forget his family, the friends he started out with, or the social conscience that had led him to write such memorable songs.

Bono went beyond participating in charitable concert events to raise money for international aid. He adopted a hands-on approach. In 1985, Bono and his wife Ali traveled to Ethiopia to help with an education and famine relief project. He particularly concentrated on raising money for Third World debts. Bono has spoken before the United Nations and the United States Congress and met with leaders such as Pope John Paul and the President of France. How many rock stars have been nominated for a Nobel Peace Prize as he was in 2003?[1]

What drives him to relentlessly continue working to end poverty and AIDs? He demonstrates that it doesn't matter if you are Catholic or Protestant or anything else—you can still make a difference in the world. Thousands of working-class fans have been inspired by his example to become involved in charitable causes. Bono's ability to inspire others is fueled by the authentic motivation of his strengths.

Looking Inside for Your Purpose

What are your deepest values? What motivates you? What is your vision, your unique legacy? How can you empower it with your character strengths? The answers require introspection and the courage to shape your own future by designing your life instead of passively letting it be determined for you. The result of this work will be a powerful sense of meaning and purpose.

I once coached a successful writer and marketer. Although she had many accomplishments, she could not shake the fear that because of her single status and the fact that her career was feast or famine, she would end up "a bag lady eating dog food" if she had no one to depend on financially. After she worked on her purpose and vision, she developed the courage and clarity to take a job in Africa as director of a nonprofit, which provides her the financial stability and long-term security she was craving. She is now incorporating her passion for writing into this new, more stable job by writing a book about her experiences. The last time we spoke she described herself as peaceful, secure, creative, and confident that things will work out.

Authentic Motivation

I've witnessed many coaching breakthroughs when the person being coached comes to understand the "why" behind his actions. It all comes down to motive. Remember when I explained the difference between talent and character strengths in chapter two? Talent is what you do well and character strengths are what you *care* to do. Understanding your motives and recognizing the unsustainable vs. sustainable sources of motivation can be a game changer. Choosing strengths motivation will provide you with authentic, sustainable motivation that gets you the most effective results. It's less about what you do and more about why you do what you do. And ultimately, discovering what you *care* to do.

So what drives you? To help my clients better understand what motivates their actions, I have developed the Motivation Grid©, based in part on the work of Dr. Paul Gilbert and my friend and colleague, Liz Patterson.[2] The Motivation Grid© helps people connect the dots from their motivation and corresponding actions to the results they are getting. As they develop awareness of what has motivated their past and present behaviors, they can intentionally choose to focus going forward on the most productive motivation that has produced the best results. The goal is to recognize when they are being motivated by character strengths (the sustainable, upward spiral) vs. counterfeits (the unsustainable, downward spiral). The three counterfeits depicted on the model are alarm, overachievement, and apathy. The alarm quadrant is characterized by fear and stress; the overachievement quadrant is characterized by perfectionism and proving self; and the apathy quadrant is characterized by hopelessness and avoidance. In contrast, the strengths quadrant is the source of sustainable motivation that enables us to make our authentic contribution in life and in work. Is your motivation getting you the results you want? Take a look at the Motivation Grid© and consider what will consistently motivate you over time to reach your potential.

Motivation Grid

ALARM Motivated by Fear: External	STRENGTHS Motivated by Authenticity: Internal
Threatened by Others	Appreciate Strengths in Self/Others
Blame/Critical	Confidence/Best Self
Fight/Flight/Freeze/Please	Autonomy/Transparency/Vulnerability
Pressure/Strain/Stress	Creativity/Flow/Focus
Anxiety/Worry	Meaning/Purpose
Danger/Threatened by Competition	Empowered yet Respectful Competitor
Lack Trust in Relationships	Bond/Build Trusting Relationships
Downward Spiral/Unsustainable *Result=Stress*	Upward Spiral/Sustainable *Result=Contribution*
OVER-ACHIEVE Motivated by Comparison: External	**APATHY** Not Motivated
Diminish/Disempower Others	Diminished by Others
Compare Self to Others/Insecurity	Hopeless/Helpless
Overdrive/Obsession/Perfectionism	Fatigue/Exhaustion/Burnout
Workaholic/Impress/Ego-Driven	Checked Out/Numb/Escape
Distraction/Overwhelm	Apathy/Don't See or Seek Solutions
Unprincipled Competitor	Insecurity/Shame/Paralyzed by Competition
Guarded/Calculating in Relationships	No Energy for Relationships
Downward Spiral/Unsustainable *Result=Proving Self*	Downward Spiral/Unsustainable *Result=Avoidance*

Goals Rarely Succeed Unless They Make Us Happy

Now that we have a handle on our motivation, we are better primed to set goals powered by character strengths. But why are goals so elusive to so many people? Millions set New Year's resolutions each January, yet experts tell us these resolutions don't work—eighty percent of people give up within six months, most within three months, and some last only days.[3] That is, unless the goals you set make you happy. Most resolutions fail because they don't make us happy while trying to achieve them. (*i.e.,* losing weight, exercising more, working harder). For most of us, in order to stick to a goal long term, it must make us happy—not the kind of happiness that comes from fleeting pleasures like buying something new, but the kind that comes from achieving something deeply important or positively impactful to others. Research shows that true happiness is rooted in a life of meaning and purpose. For example, the good feeling we get when we express our strengths will keep us energized as we work on our goals. Attaching a goal to something bigger than ourselves empowers the goal.

> There is a principle that what we focus on grows, so if we're focused on "not eating chocolate cake" then chocolate cake will become our obsession.

As we learned earlier, when we shift from no to yes, we are more focused and empowered. This is because when we focus on what we *want* instead of what we *don't want,* we have a vision of the action we will take. A goal will have a much greater chance of success if it is truly meaningful to us, helps others we care about, and—most importantly—if we are working *toward* something rather than denying ourselves by staying *away* from something. There is a principle that what we focus on grows, so if we're focused on "not eating chocolate cake," then chocolate cake will become our obsession.

Willpower vs. Fortitude

In my many years coaching people to achieve their goals, I was somewhat surprised to learn that developing willpower is not the main ingredient in sustainable change. Willpower is the ability to forego something you really want in the moment—like that second piece of chocolate cake or spending money earmarked for bills on a new distraction. What really matters in the change process is developing the fortitude, or internal strength, to self-regulate. I can develop fortitude by *planning* for the overwhelming desire I know I will experience when I see my favorite chocolate cake's glistening frosting beckoning me like an old friend. The plan might be filling myself with a satisfying, healthy meal or satiating snacks that I truly enjoy, and then taking the time to sit and slowly savor just one piece of cake instead of two or three.

Research shows that when people exercise willpower to deny themselves of something they love, they eventually will be much more prone to indulge in something else later on.[4] This fact explains why deprivation doesn't work over time. The key is to find a substitute that we love even more than the taste of chocolate cake to anchor the new behavior, such as the reward that we are getting healthy for those we love, including the self-love we are developing in the process. Saying yes to something else we want most is much more powerful than saying no to ourselves. That slight shift in thinking causes our actions to leave us feeling nurtured instead of deprived and denied.

"Be" a Contribution

Back to the New Year's resolutions—another reason many fail is because they are focused only on self. Without the tie to others, such as shown in the strengths quadrant of the Motivation Grid©, those resolutions don't have enough long-term motivation to keep us going. We thrive when those around us thrive. If I see myself as being a "contribution" to others rather than just accomplishing a goal for myself, then whatever I do is powered by something bigger than myself. As I apply my strengths to the goal process, I am bringing my authentic, best self to the work; and this energizes me. I am no longer distracted by alarm, overachievement, or apathy because I am focused instead on contributing my best work through my strengths. Creating value and fulfillment for the recipient of my contribution in turn creates value and fulfillment for me, launching a positive upward spiral. It's the law of reciprocity—what goes around comes around.

"Being" a Contribution:

1. Fills you with meaning and purpose

2. Energizes your goal as you use your strengths

3. Serves as an antidote for unproductive competition and comparison

4. Creates value and fulfillment for the recipient of your actions and thus you

If your goal is to lose weight or exercise, ask yourself, "Why do I want to do this?" Which is more compelling: losing twenty pounds to look better or becoming healthy so that you have more energy to participate in fun activities with those you love? If you see yourself as a contribution to your family, then getting and staying healthy becomes deeply compelling—and you will be far more motivated and likely to accomplish it. The TV show, The Biggest Loser, is a great example of this. Notice the people who are most successful in accomplishing their weight loss goal on the show. Most often they are the ones who are motivated by themes in the strengths quadrant of the Motivation Grid©—such as building relationships, being their best self, living a life of meaning and purpose. For example, they think about how weight loss will allow them to better serve their families and friends, to be around to see their kids grow up, to inspire their loved ones to get healthy, to better enjoy activities with friends, or to have the energy to contribute to others. Instead of anchoring their goal in what they must "give up," such as favorite foods, they anchor their goals in what they will "gain," such as energy, longevity, enhanced relationships and meaningful contributions to others.

When we work from the desire to make things better for others, obstacles seem to vanish and unpleasant tasks become more pleasant. Those negative, critical, judging internal voices in the alarm quadrant of the Motivation Grid©, and our ego's desire for outdoing others in the overachievement quadrant fall away. We focus only on what we want to give—it becomes a freeing and joyful experience. I remember the first time I had a television appearance as an "expert coach." As I drove to the TV station, my clammy hands gripped the steering wheel and I could feel my heart pounding in my chest as I mentally reviewed what I would say. I took a couple of deep breaths and said out loud, "Fatima, just 'be a contribution' today. Think only about helping people today, and everything will fall into place."

That small motivation adjustment transported me from fear of failure to simply wanting to get helpful information across to people. Like everyone, I get caught up in everyday pressures to perform; but when I'm immersed in using my character strengths to contribute, the performance anxiety melts away; and I get the deep satisfaction that comes from giving to others. The world becomes a much less complicated place.

Your Strengths Plan

The intent of strengths coaching is to create a practical and positive action plan going forward. "What's the plan?" How many times have you heard that question from your spouse, friends or colleagues? Plans reassure people. Use the following strengths coaching principles when developing a strengths plan.

1. In the Driver's Seat: No one is more interested in your growth than you. The person being coached should always do the "heavy lifting" by offering solutions and using "I" language to vocalize their own agenda.

2. Strengths Focus: Use the steps on the following page for feedback/feedforward. Frame all feedback through the positive lens of strengths. Shift quickly from feedback to solution-oriented feedforward to envision a better future.

3. Positive Change: Model new and better behaviors consistently over time to build trust. Transform old thinking/patterns/labels that no longer serve you into strengths-aligned behaviors. The key is to be patient while keeping your eyes on the goal.

Feedback and Feedforward

It is more inspiring and productive to help people learn to be "strong" than to point out where they are "wrong." Let's get real! Most people dread feedback because traditional feedback can be threatening, often anchoring a negative self-image and self-fulfilling prophecies. We can, however, learn to quickly redirect feedback through a constructive lens by identifying strengths to address issues. Next, we should focus most of our time and energy on motivating feedforward, which identifies ideas and solutions to achieve goals as we visualize our ideal future.

Strengths-Focused Feedback

The first step in selecting our highest leverage goal(s) is framing feedback through the constructive lens of strengths as outlined below:

- Acknowledge feedback and thank those who gave it to you. Balance feedback by acknowledging strengths first, then growth opportunities.

- Laser your goal focus. Look for patterns in the feedback, and if you see a theme you believe is accurate, choose a strengths-powered goal to address it.

- Shift quickly to feedforward.

Strengths-Focused Feedforward

- Reflect on past successes in which you were at your best, and explore the factors that enabled the successes. Use what worked best for you to create positive practices going forward.

- Brainstorm potential goals. If you could wave a magic wand to improve your situation, what would change? If you expressed your strengths more consistently, how would that affect your situation?

- Using the STRONG Visualization© technique you learned in Chapter 3, vividly and with great detail imagine using your strengths to create your ideal situation. Visualize it at relevant milestones, such as one month, six months or one year from now.

Shifting to Feedforward

Though it would be ideal to focus exclusively on feedforward, the reality is that we will be met with feedback throughout our lives. Yet, we have the power to quickly shift our focus to feedforward. Sometimes, the best we can do is be our own advocate when others in our lives remain feedback-focused. However, our focus on feedforward can inspire others to shift to feedforward as well. Here is an example of a husband and wife who experienced this shift:

"My husband and I were at the airport looking for parking so we could embark on a vacation. My husband turned into the service area by accident, which potentially could have resulted in us missing our flight. I vocalized my concern, which increased the stress both of us were feeling in that moment. He snapped back at me. It was easy to see we were on the verge of an argument, potentially ruining a beautiful trip.

"Once we finally parked, we boarded the shuttle and my husband quite obviously sat apart from me. He was definitely giving me feedback with his body language. My pattern in the past would have been to discuss the situation in detail with feedback phrases like: 'I felt frustrated when you...' or 'When you did (this), it made me feel like (this).' But on this day, I had an 'Aha!' moment. What if I used feedforward instead? What if I focused on what I loved about him rather than spend the next hour 'processing' what we had both done wrong? I was excited to try it out. I thanked him for loading my bag onto the shuttle and for driving to the airport. I was surprised when he thanked me back for planning the trip! One positive focus continued to generate another as we appreciated one another's strengths, until we were both relaxed, smiling and using feedforward to envision a great trip together!"

This story demonstrates the impact feedforward can have on a relationship. It also shows how one person's choice to focus on feedforward can shift the dynamic.

Feedforward is also a powerful tool to use at work—particularly as a leader. Statistics tell us that the number one reason people leave their work positions is because they quit their boss—not the job.

A common practice in the workplace is for employees to undergo a performance review. A coaching client of mine observed the difference between two managers she worked under and created two lists outlining those differences. Note the two boxes below, which detail how Manager A focused more on feedforward and Manager B focused more on feedback—and the difference in their results.

Manager A Performance Review Process	Manager B Performance Review Process
• *Feedforward Focus: 90% of meeting* What is going strong and how to continue to leverage strengths moving forward, as well as how to build underused strengths moving forward.	• *Feedforward Focus: 10% of meeting* What is going strong is mentioned briefly as meeting begins, only as a precursor to the more important discussion of what's wrong.

Feedback Focus: 10% of meeting Necessary feedback quickly shifts to feedforward opportunities for building underused strengths. Employee is encouraged to lead the conversation.	*Feedback Focus: 90% of meeting* Majority of time spent analyzing what is going wrong and needs to be fixed. Conversation is led by manager.
• *Collaborative Communication* Employee's <u>willingness</u> to discuss necessary improvements directly correlates to trust level with manager (high trust). Employee <u>safely</u> discusses areas where improvement is needed and participates in a collaborative brainstorming session with manager about how to turn these into future strengths.	• *Defensive Communication* Employee's <u>unwillingness</u> to discuss necessary improvements directly correlates to trust level with manager (low trust). Employee's feeling of <u>unsafety</u> leads to defensive communication, including overemphasis on excuses/reasons for mistakes rather than focusing on how to turn them into future strengths.
• *STRONG Goals*© Goals are set based on building underused strengths and leveraging top strengths.	• *Feedback Focus: 90% of meeting* Goals are set based on providing regular evidence of a discontinuance of mistakes.
• *Monthly Meetings: Strengths-Building* Monthly meetings are scheduled to discuss ongoing opportunities to leverage top strengths and to build underused strengths.	• *Monthly Meetings: Evidence of Compliance* Monthly meetings are scheduled to provide evidence of goal compliance with emphasis on discontinuance of mistakes.
• *Message sent by Manager A:* "What can I do to help you succeed?"	• *Message sent by Manager B:* "You're not measuring up."
• *Message received by employee:* "I have value. I am worthy."	• *Message received by employee:* "I'm not safe. I'm not worthy."
Manager A = Advocate	**Manager B = Compliance Officer**

After creating these two lists, my coaching client reflected on what she learned from the experience of working under each of the managers:

"While working at my place of employment, I enjoyed high job satisfaction under Manager A, then began experiencing a snowball effect of unhappiness at work under Manager B. It actually became intolerable enough that I began to consider seeking employment elsewhere (after investing fifteen years in this job). After learning about feedback and feedforward, I recognized that my job satisfaction was DIRECTLY related to the way I was being perceived and valued by these two managers rather than tied to any lack of personal satisfaction with the work itself. This insight marked a dramatic shift for me! This led me to a significant insight related to my own focus of control. Though I was still working under Manager B, who was not in the regular habit of focusing on what was strong in me, *I could provide that positive focus for myself.* I could practice feedforward, both personally AND in my interactions with Manager B. This insight helped me shift my focus and start recognizing (again) the many things I loved about my job. And, though far from perfect, my relationship with Manager B is improving incrementally. Most importantly, my personal focus on feedforward helps me to regularly recognize strengths in myself, thus increasing my feelings of value and worth from within."

STRONG Goals© Tool

After reframing feedback positively and using the feedforward technique, you are ready to set one or two high leverage goals. I have developed a tool for the strengths based goal attainment process I use with my coaching clients. It is the acronym STRONG with each letter representing a critical phase in reaching any goal.

Here is a description of each of the six phases of STRONG Goals©:

1. **Strengths**: Empower your goal by identifying which of your strengths will help you accomplish the goal. Build around what has worked well–drawing from past successes in which you were at your best, identifying the strengths that enabled achievements, intentionally recreating success going forward. As you apply your strengths to the goal, you are bringing your authentic, best self to the work-- this will energize the goal and you!

2. **Timed**: Ensure that your goal has clearly defined timeframes or milestones that allow you to check progress along the way. Build confidence through small, consistent gains. Plan realistic celebrations for each milestone.

3. **Relevant**: Give the goal long-term relevance by infusing it with meaning and purpose. Consider the contribution you want to make for yourself and for others. Goals tied to others, especially our important relationships, produce long-term motivation and enthusiasm—we thrive when those around us thrive. If we see ourselves as being a "contribution" to others rather than just accomplishing a goal for self, then our efforts are relevant long term—powered by something larger than self. Start with a clear picture in your mind, using your senses, visualizing in great detail how your strengths will be used to accomplish your goal and the impact it will have on you and others. Write it down or have pictures represent it, making the description as vivid as possible.

4. **Options**: Weigh all your options. Explore the potential rewards and costs of each of your goal options so that you can choose the highest leverage goal to focus on. Don't overload—choose one realistic goal at a time to focus on.

5. **Network**: Identify a support network. Have you identified all available resources (people, education, financial, etc.)? Assess the ability of family members, friends, peers and other contacts to provide support.

6. **Growth**: Grow with a goal that stretches and inspires you. Reflect on progress, reveal insights and recalibrate when necessary. Reflect on progress by asking, "How did I get closer to my goal and how can I remove obstacles?" As you reveal insights to help you reach your goal, recalibrate when needed. Recalibration takes into consideration unforeseen changes in your circumstances that may require a new approach or a change in goal. Be honest with yourself and open to growth.

Focus on Strengths

As we learned earlier, though human nature appears wired to focus on our faults, life is more fulfilling and we're more likely to perform well when we focus on our strengths. When we view our strengths as a gift we can apply to a need, the dynamic shifts. Using our strengths is motivating because people *enjoy* using their gifts. People who use their strengths are six times as likely to be engaged and three times as likely to report an excellent quality of life.[5]

Sometimes people are hesitant to state their strengths out loud. It's time to create environments where people are encouraged to acknowledge their strengths. We can learn to share our strengths in the spirit of contribution, which takes the "ego" out of the equation and becomes our unique way to contribute to the betterment of the whole. The following words from Nelson Mandela's inaugural address are a call to action for each of us to leverage our strengths for the collective whole: "Your playing small does not serve the world. There is nothing enlightened about shrinking so that other people won't feel insecure around you. We are all meant to shine... It's not in just some of us; it's in everyone. As we let our own light shine, we unconsciously give others permission to do the same."[6]

Once you connect to your authentic strengths motivation, you are fueled to live your values and embrace your vision and purpose.[7] As you contribute your best self, you will feel more connected and operate more effectively in the world around you.

Dr. Edgar Mitchell, Apollo 14 astronaut and the sixth man to walk on the moon, is said to have described the experience of realizing his mission and feeling at one with the universe this way: "The biggest joy was on the way home. In my cockpit window I saw the earth, the moon, and the sun, and the whole 360° panoramic of the heavens. That was a powerful, overwhelming experience...And that was an overwhelming sense of oneness and connectedness."[8]

But you don't have to go to those lengths to understand and fulfill your purpose. You can be one with the world even with the pull of gravity nipping at your heels!

Coaching Tip

With our overstuffed schedules, finding time to contemplate meaningful questions can be difficult. These questions are foundational to setting goals empowered by strengths. Give yourself the gift of space to answer them fully. Encourage all whom you are coaching to do the same.

STRONG Questions©: Motivation

- What are the strengths I most admire in others?
- Which of my strengths increase appreciation of self/others?
- Which of my strengths develop transparency/ vulnerability/ accountability?
- Which of my strengths increase meaning/purpose?
- Which of my strengths increase confidence/my best self?
- Which of my strengths increase creativity/flow/focus?
- How will I discover new ways to make my contribution?
- What constructive feedback inspires me to change?
- Which of my strengths do others confirm?
- What strengths am I blind to in myself?
- What are my top three goals? What strengths align with and empower my goals?
- If I had a "magic wand," what things would change?

When you are content to be
simply yourself and don't
care or compete,
everybody will

RESPECT

you

Lao Tsu

6 | COMPARANOIA

"Comparison is the death of joy."

—Mark Twain

"Insecurity comes from comparing our out-take scenes with everyone else's highlight reel."

—Anonymous

Brazilian marathon runner Vanderlei de Lima had a ninety-second lead at the Athens Olympic games in 2004 when a man appeared out of nowhere and pushed de Lima into the crowd. He lost thirty seconds of his time and never quite recovered his focus. Shaken—later he said he thought the man was going to kill him—he was overtaken by two runners and ended up winning only the bronze medal instead of the gold. Nevertheless, he celebrated upon entering the stadium, blowing kisses to the fans.

"For me it wasn't important if it was gold, silver, or bronze," de Lima said on his return to Brazil where he'd been a peasant farm worker by the age of eight and often didn't have enough to eat. "The most important thing was to make it to the podium."

That moment of ecstasy and happiness was bigger than the frustration of missing out on the gold because of a deranged man's actions. Later he said that overcoming the man's attack and having to struggle for the bronze made him appreciate it that much more. If he had focused on a loss he could not control, he would have also lost the magic of the podium experience.

His acceptance of his fate, when he had been so close to becoming the first person to win a gold medal for Brazil in the men's marathon, was so inspirational he was awarded the Pierre de Coubertin medal for Sportsmanship at the closing ceremony.

Vanderlei de Lima didn't look at what he had lost to two other runners, but at what he had won for himself. He did not fall into the trap of complaining or being cynical. The runner was competing, to be sure, but he did not get sucked into the unhealthy territory of competing to prove his sense of worth in comparison to others. In fact, his fellow athletes were so impressed with the way he conducted himself that Emanuel Rego, who won the gold medal in volleyball, gave his gold medal to de Lima, who promptly returned it: "I can't accept Emanuel's medal. I'm happy with mine; it's bronze but means gold," said Vanderlei.

Comparing our own progress or success with others' successes has been characterized as "keeping up with the Joneses," based on a comic strip that originated in the U.S. in the early 1900s. In it, a never-seen neighboring family was portrayed as having a bigger house, greener lawn, better furnishings, more success at work, nicer children, an enviable couples relationship—all the things any family would want for themselves. Every culture has its own version of social envy, the "green-eyed monster" that keeps people striving for things they don't really need because those things are perceived as status symbols.

There's nothing wrong with healthy competition in sports or the marketplace, or with healthy comparisons we make for purposes of learning. What is unhealthy is when competition and comparison turn into judgment that diminishes self and others. Working for material rather than personal goals can lead to alienation in the workforce as employees look over their shoulders to compare themselves against others in a competition to see who will win and who will lose.

After professional photographer Kevin Garrett lost several jobs photographing for record labels in Nashville to celebrity shooter Andrew Eccles, he noticed that his competitor was slated to teach a course at the Santa Fe Photographic Workshops. He signed up, paying several thousand dollars and turning down a big job that came up the day before the workshop was starting. The opportunity to be coached on his craft was more important.

"Two hours into the workshop, I saw so clearly why I wasn't getting the jobs and he was," recalled Garrett. "He was so generous in showing us photos, his favorite lighting setups. He withheld nothing. That week changed my life."

Garrett took what the famed photographer said to heart. "When I'm being paid at the level I'm paid, I must be able to produce a memorable image on demand," Garrett said. "The account executive, the art director, and the client are all watching your raw images come up on the screen. You cannot let the pressure get to you. Andrew coached me on the importance of making the entire experience fun by thinking through all the details from the music playing to the craft services. It's all important."

In the ensuing year, Garrett's income tripled, all because he was willing to open himself to coaching from a competitor. "Shortly after spending that week with Andrew, I was shooting a magazine cover in a studio," said Garrett. "The studio manager came in and said, 'I've been working here for years, and I've never seen such a beautiful lighting setup.'" Garrett silently thanked his former competitor, whom he had enlisted as his coach.

Comparanoia

When comparison turns from perceptive discernments to discriminating judgments that rank things, it becomes a fear-based pursuit that separates people into categories rather than unites them as a team. When, instead of looking for uniting factors such as what we can learn from another person who is good at what we do, we look instead for what makes us better or worse than someone else, we contribute to the illusion that we are more different than alike. With this kind of

When comparison turns from perceptive discernments to discriminating judgements that rank things, it becomes a fear-based pursuit that separates people.

thinking, we reaffirm the fallacy that human worth can be distilled into comparisons. Ultimately, "comparanoia," a trendy, made-up word that means excessive comparing, is much like racism in its consequences. Someone must be better because they have more or are more; and someone must be worse because they have less or what they do or are is "less than."

Women, especially, are familiar with comparing themselves with others from an early age. Our culture's message to girls is all about appearance and body image and judging ourselves in terms of others: "I'm not as slim as other girls" or "I'm not in a committed relationship as all happy women should be." Boys endure a similar challenge in the arena of athletics and success in business. Both men and women compare their earnings not only to others, but often within their own couple relationships: "I'm not as successful as my career women friends because I choose to stay home and raise my children," or "I'm a loser because my wife makes more money than me."

Many of us gather our ideas from the pages of magazines and images on television ads. When we buy what the media is selling instead of what we believe based on our own values, we live by flawed pop culture standards and see ourselves through a distorted lens. In other words, we lose our freedom to express ourselves. We silence our own voices and even our own thoughts in an effort to compete in someone else's race. This is not the path to greatness.

In the extreme, comparanoia can lead to widespread economic ruin. "Living above one's means" is rampant based on credit card usage.[1] According to the U.S. Federal Reserve, more than forty percent of households spend more than they earn.[2] Many financial institutions and other traditionally reliable industries have failed in part due to competitive greed.

It is more important than ever to train people to be co-creators of prosperity and abundance rather than to look over their shoulders to see who can outrun whom. Focusing on and appreciating strengths is the opposite of comparanoia because it is focusing on what we and others do well. It celebrates everyone's unique character strengths combinations and the contributions to the whole that result from those strengths.

Through this cooperative and appreciative diversity, each of us is more productive overall.

Strengths Coaching: Striving Together

The original meaning of the verb "to compete" is "competere," which means "to strive together." Today however, many of us think of competition in terms of rivals and contention. In 2004, Kevin Garrett, the photographer mentioned above, suffered a mild traumatic brain injury when his car was struck from the rear on his way to a photo shoot. David Johnson, another photographer Garrett had met at the Santa Fe Workshop, learned about the car wreck and that Garrett was having difficulties. He cleared his schedule and flew from his studio in New York to help Garrett learn how to use some new equipment.

After reviewing Garrett's portfolio, he gently chided him for using the quality and popularity of his past work as his benchmark. "I know you're in pain," he said. "But you've flattened out creatively. The best photographs of your life need to be the things you shoot today and the images you will shoot tomorrow." Garrett thanked Johnson for his honesty and for caring enough to speak up.

A great strengths coach is willing to give constructive feedback that isn't always what the other person wants to hear. Pointing out when strengths have atrophied and need attention is not easy. Calling forth your character strengths when surrounded by colleagues who have traded in character for winning at all costs can require courage. That type of coaching relationship is possible only when a high level of trust is present. Professional photography is known to be a cutthroat business and, over the years, Johnson and Garrett have gone on to compete directly for jobs at times. They've astonished some of their clients by recommending each other for jobs, loaning each other equipment, and sharing names of crew members in a business where people jealously guard every aspect of their business.

> A great strengths coach is willing to give constructive feedback that isn't always what the other person wants to hear.

One of the iconic examples of camaraderie was Fernando Diaz and Antonio Cánovas in the Madrid Marathon. The two friends and running companions had competed for the lead throughout the race, but as they neared the finish line, Cánovas was racked with muscle cramps. Diaz threw his arm around Cánovas and helped his faltering rival across the finish line first. The judges ruled Cánovas the winner. The two runners shared the prize money and both advanced to the Boston marathon. The generosity of the gesture between competitors far outweighed any prize.

If we could see those around us as co-creators in our growth, gravitating toward them and learning that another's star quality doesn't dim our own brightness, we might learn that we can all shine more brilliantly. Great coaches are basically high achievers who see themselves as resources rather than competitors.

Hold Up a Mirror to Strengths

Learning to appreciate character strengths does not diminish self or others, but rather builds people, teams, and organizations. When we strive to develop what is noble and best in ourselves, others will catch the vision and want to do the same. In fact, Seligman and Peterson described the impact of character strengths as follows:

> In many if not most cases, onlookers are elevated by their observation of virtuous action. Admiration is created more than jealousy because character strengths are the sorts of characteristics to which most can—and do—aspire. The more people surrounding us who are kind, or curious, or full of hope, the greater our own likelihood of acting in these ways. Said another way, strengths accompany non-zero sum games (Wright, 1999). All are winners when someone acts in accordance with his or her strengths and virtues.[3]

The coach's task is to listen and respond to a client's distinctive voice. Without our own voices, we risk an authoritarian kind of existence, with unacceptable standards imposed upon us because we did not speak up. The old model of coaching was to be a judge, magnifying weaknesses under a microscope so defects could be addressed and overall performance improved. The new model of coaching is to hold up a mirror to strengths, to take the best that is already there and leverage it. A strengths coach's job is to make sure people are focused on their own vision and potential, not someone else's.

I coached a woman who had decided to leave the corporate world to stay home with her children. She enjoyed her children, but fretted that her friends were leaping ahead of her in their careers. When her children were in kindergarten, she decided to re-evaluate. She didn't want to punch a clock and miss their childhood, but she also believed she had skills and creativity seeking expression. Rather than staying in the position of comparing herself to her friends or limiting herself by either/or thinking, we explored her signature strengths—the strengths that gave her the most energy and inspiration when she used them. This jump-started an entirely new realm of exploration for her. She began to clarify her vision of her ideal future powered by her signature strengths. I could see her come to life as she thought about the exciting possibilities she hadn't considered before, all the while staying grounded by weighing the rewards and costs of each option.

> A strengths coach's job is to make sure people are focused on their own vision and potential, not someone else's.

My client, through visualizing her ideal future and using STRONG Questions© to elicit the best possible scenario, created the optimal business that would allow her to have the family-oriented lifestyle she wanted and also utilize her creative energy. She realized she could afford a slow and steady pace, which is something that many of her friends did not have the luxury of in their corporate jobs. Rather than just operating on the basis of the old-fashioned pros and cons list, she explored her strengths and creatively designed what she wanted: a successful marketing and consulting business that she works on while the kids are at school.

Ben Zander (the orchestra conductor in chapter one) encourages his musicians to "lead from every chair." Often a musician or employee will feel like second fiddle to someone else's outstanding star qualities. A smart strengths coach, like an attuned conductor, will get the message across that there is no such thing as second fiddle with strengths. An orchestra, a team, and a company are made up of elements that must all pull their weight and work together in order for the whole to perform at its peak. A strengths coach neither overshadows nor compares, but pinpoints the unique character strengths that elevate talents and rocket a person to new heights.

Coaching Tip

Be curious. Never underestimate the power of questions. The answers are there. Remember the best way to learn something is to share it with someone else.

STRONG Questions©: Relationships

- How can I best use my signature strengths to create positive relationships?
- What strengths can I build/develop further to encourage better cooperation in my relationships?
- How will I benefit by letting go of unproductive competitive feelings toward others?
- What strategies will I use to refrain from comparing myself to others?
- How can I look for a solution that benefits everyone?
- Are there any strengths that I might be using in ways that unintentionally cause problems or strengths collisions? How?
- How can I best balance meeting my needs while respecting the needs of others?

Emotional consequences stem
not directly from adversity
but from one's

BELIEFS

about adversity.

Dr. Martin P. Seligman

7 | REFRAME FAILURE

"No one can go back and make a brand new start, my friend;
but anyone can start from here and make a brand new end."

—Dan Zadra

I did not look forward to a long stay at my mother's home after my brother's untimely death. I felt such a deep sadness and emotional vulnerability, especially since it had been only two years since my father's passing. My mother's bouts with debilitating illness had sometimes caused our roles to be reversed when I was a child. Not wanting to burden her with my childhood worries and adolescent challenges, I had kept my youthful insecurities to myself and trudged on.

But after the catharsis of the funeral, I decided to look for all that I could appreciate and embrace about my childhood. I already knew that I loved my parents deeply, that they had done the best they could, and that there were so many things to admire about them. I also knew that the time had come to let go of my expectations and celebrate all the growth opportunities my childhood had provided me. What a healing and miraculous experience I enjoyed once I decided to focus only on the positive!

I opened my eyes and saw a spry, energetic, intelligent woman who loves animals, reading, plants, cooking, and who prays the rosary each night. I observed a woman who gravitates toward anything that represents life, creativity, and nature. I recalled the time a wild squirrel ate peacefully out of her hand. She had a genuine goodness and strength about her. She was an interesting woman, a different woman than the one lodged in my consciousness, the mother of my memory tape.

My regrets melted away, and I enjoyed our time together without judgment. The difference in how I felt about my childhood was simply a matter of perspective. The shift was dependent on my point of view.

At times when I looked into the dark tunnel of my childhood, I felt like a train was coming at me and the only safety was cringing against a wall. This time the light was not from a locomotive bearing down on me; it was the sun shining through the other end of the tunnel. All I had to do was follow the light and walk out of the past into a different place. That's where I found my wonderful mother.

> **Remember that sometimes gifts come wrapped in the most unlikely packages.**

Most parents do the best they can with what they have been given. The trap that I fell into is a common one. It is seductive to blame people, circumstances and events—to get stuck in the regrets. Most of us could benefit from looking back on hard times and asking ourselves how we can best reframe those experiences through a more accurate, appreciative, and positive lens. Remember that sometimes gifts come wrapped in the most unlikely packages.

The Power of Perception

"I've missed more than 9,000 shots in my career. I've lost almost 300 games. Twenty-six times, I've been trusted to take the game- winning shot and missed. I've failed over and over and over again in my life. And that is why I succeed." —Michael Jordan[1]

Inarguably, Michael Jordan is the greatest basketball player of all time. And yet he has modeled for the world that setbacks are part of success. What if we stopped considering our setbacks as set-ups for failure? What if we could come to see that deficiency is often part of an overall proficiency?

Some of the world's greatest thinkers and leaders were told that they would never amount to anything or were labeled due to disabilities. Sir Richard Branson, founder of more than 100 companies in his Virgin empire and one of the world's great philanthropists, has dyslexia and performed poorly in school, dropping out at the age of sixteen. Both Thomas Edison, who still holds more patents than anyone, and Albert Einstein performed poorly in traditional schools and were allegedly homeschooled by their mothers; each woman was reportedly told that her son suffered from retardation. These divergent thinkers used their problem-solving skills to dream up groundbreaking solutions, inventions, and services. In Thomas Edison's words, "Many of life's failures are people who did not realize how close they were to success when they gave up. I have not failed. I've just found 10,000 ways that won't work."[2]

Victim or Victor?

"While victimization creates dependency and distrust, accountability creates interdependence and trust," says Stephen M.R. Covey in *The Speed of Trust*.[3] When a leader, team member, or family member takes responsibility, it encourages others to do the same.

But sometimes people get stuck in the victim role and can't move ahead. It takes imagination to envision something different and better than the limiting stories we have been telling ourselves our whole lives, whether they are echoes of others' voices or our own inner critic. You may have heard the acronym FEAR, which maps to False Evidence Appearing Real. Often the stories we have internalized are not based on our reality, but on someone else's distortion. Choosing a new, more accurate story to tell yourself, stepping back and allowing powerful new questions and gratitude to enter into the process, defuses victim mentality. Amplifying a positive voice gives power and energy to our authentic self, guiding us to the heart of all matters.

Breaking the Chain

First of all, suffering at some points in our lives is not necessarily a negative thing. "Suffering is a great equalizer. You have a choice to let it make you better or bitter," says my colleague Sam Bracken. "That one letter makes all the difference in how you approach life."

Who would have thought that when Bracken's mother said to him at age fifteen, "I don't want you anymore; you get in the way of my partying—you have to leave," that her abandonment of him would turn out to be his chance to become a victor? A family from his church took him in, which allowed him a glimpse of what a normal home life looked like. He took his childhood suffering and leveraged it by inspiring others who had suffered hardship. As a motivational speaker and author of *My Orange Duffel Bag: A Journey to Radical Change*, he is on a mission to help homeless young people, high poverty youth, and teens aging out of foster care, see that they can change—no matter their circumstances. As I often say to those I coach: you can acknowledge your story, but then use your character strengths to start to build a new and better story. You don't have to stick to the script that others have written for you.

Lighting a path out of a past obscured by the darkness of failure is part of what defines a great coach or leader in any setting. Your willingness to inspire others to forge a new beginning by breaking past negative patterns inspires hope. Listening attentively to the concerns and burdens of another, all the while communicating your belief in their ability to grow from the situation, can move a weakness to a strength and significantly bolster your coaching relationship. When we look deeply into another person's potential, we are showing respect. The word "respect" literally means to "look again," or in other words, to "appreciate" their unique strengths.

While I was at a strengths coaching workshop, one of the instructors shared his experience of being hijacked in a dark Brooklyn parking garage. He was walking to his car at night after having taught a yoga class. Suddenly three teenagers approached him, and he felt a gun pressed to his back. They forced him into the back seat of his car. One teenager climbed in with him and kept the gun on him. The other two got in the front, and they sped away.

He had a full-blown panic attack in the back of his car as they sped recklessly through city streets. Soon they ran a couple of red lights in quick succession. He slowly calmed himself with some deep breathing from his yoga training and told them, "If you keep running red lights, the police are going to chase us and it's not going to end very pretty."

They slowed down and started talking to him. "You look like us," they said. As he regained his composure, he decided to use his strengths training and asked them, "What are you good at?" The leader let a string of obscenities fly, but my colleague persisted with his questions: "No, I mean what are you really good at? What do you love to do?"

Once they realized he was genuinely interested, they settled down and said, "We're good at hip hop. We like to move our bodies, and we like rhythm. We even write some lyrics sometimes." They then put a baseball cap on his head and taught him some hip-hop moves, making him dance in the back seat with the gun at the small of his back. After a forty-five-minute joy ride, they left him in a dark alley on a Brooklyn street and drove off.

The interesting thing about this story is that the next day the police found his car, which was almost brand-new, completely undamaged with his laptop right where he'd left it in the car. He concluded his story by saying, "We are asking the wrong questions of people. We are asking 'What's wrong with you?' instead of asking 'What's right with you?'"

> We are asking "What's wrong with you?" instead of asking "What's right with you?"

Letting Go

To many of us, forgiveness is tantamount to surrendering a battle. But once we realize that we contribute to our own suffering by holding on to negativity, we can see the wisdom in letting go. I once heard someone say, "Holding on to anger is like taking poison and expecting the other person to die." Letting go is freeing.

Often in business we have to let go of an idea or a program or a brand that is not working. We hold on tight and fight for what we think is right. Then when we lose, we hold a grudge or sabotage progress to show we don't agree with the outcome. A coach's task is to guide people beyond this level. The sooner we forgive and free ourselves to move on, the less likely we are to become or remain a victim.

Shining a light on our dark and negative thoughts can lessen the shadows they cast and free us to make better choices. It's as simple, in a way, as crossing to the sunny side of a street.

Reframing Failure

We do not have to look far to find examples of people who have found ways to reframe a failure in their lives. I have a friend who had successfully practiced law for twenty years. He had been a partner and the president of a large firm and held leadership positions in the American Bar Association. He was one of the lawyers who had obtained the first civil antitrust settlement from Microsoft in the early 2000s, reported to be hundreds of millions of dollars. The success continued for Ryan until the last startup company he worked with was forced into bankruptcy.

The friends and colleagues he worked with at the company were either laid off or they were compelled to find other employment. Ryan stayed on with the company, but was deeply discouraged as the prospects for the company, its customers, and himself dwindled away. Ryan explains, "At about the time I was trying to decide whether to stay on or leave, someone sent me a link to a YouTube video highlighting the final collegiate football game I was involved in for Brigham Young University—the 1980 Holiday Bowl between BYU and Southern Methodist University. The clip was uploaded by CBS Sports and has been viewed hundreds of thousands of times. The video chronicles how SMU pounded BYU for at least three and a half quarters in that Bowl game. The game started out 19 to 7 for SMU at the end of the first quarter and, with about three minutes to go in the game, the score stood at 45 to 25 for SMU. Many of the BYU fans left the San Diego stadium in shame and discouragement, assuming it would be a blowout win for SMU.

Led by future NFL star quarterback Jim McMahon, BYU overcame that 45 – 25 deficit in the last three minutes of the game and then, with no time on the clock, BYU won the game on a fifty-yard "Hail Mary" pass. That game has come to be known as "The Miracle Bowl" and is consistently listed as one of the greatest, improbable Bowl comebacks of all time—even over thirty years later. The McMahon to Brown Hail Mary pass is identified by Wikipedia as a prime example of what a Hail Mary pass is.

When Ryan watched the YouTube clip of the Miracle Bowl, he was reminded of what he and his teammates learned that night in San Diego: No matter how bleak things look, no matter how discouraged you are, never quit—never ever give up. So, that made his decision for him—he couldn't quit; but what was he supposed to do with problem after problem and failure after failure for his company—it did look hopeless. "I waited over thirty years for someone to write a book about the miraculous Miracle Bowl comeback, but no one did, so I finally decided, 'Why not me?'" he explains.

The result of this process of reframing failure for Ryan is his best-selling book *Hail Mary—The Inside Story of BYU's 1980 Miracle Bowl Comeback*. He reframed his failure by turning the story that inspired him to weather his business failure into a best-selling book that has also been picked up and turned into an inspirational DVD by the same name. Ryan explains further, "I knew I did not want to totally abandon my company and the investors and lawyers who had asked me to help guide them through the troubled waters, but I also knew that if I did not find something else meaningful and interesting to do, I would become despondent. The research and writing of that book and reconnecting with teammates and coaches from that 1980 Miracle Bowl team was another miracle during those years of stress and failure with my company." He also used one other type of inspiration during this time of "failure." He said he has loved the poem *IF* by Rudyard Kipling since he had to memorize it in junior high school. When he was trying to decide whether to write the book, he thought of the lines from that poem that read, "If you can fill the unforgiving minute with sixty seconds' worth of distance run, yours is the Earth and everything that's in it," and that inspired him to start his book. Ryan believes that *Hail Mary* is his sixty seconds worth of distance run.

Recovering from Failure: Post-Traumatic Growth

"Success is the ability to go from failure to failure without losing your enthusiasm."

—*Winston Churchill*

In "Building Resilience," a 2011 *Harvard Business Review* article[4], Dr. Martin Seligman tells of two MBA graduates, Douglas and Walter, who were laid off by their Wall Street companies during an economic downturn. Both reeled from the blow, experiencing depression and anxiety. For Douglas, the trauma was short-lived. After two weeks he told himself, "It's not me; it's the economy going through a bad patch. I'm good at what I do, and there will be a market for my skills." He updated his résumé and sent it to a dozen New York firms, all of which rejected him. He then tried six companies in his Ohio hometown and eventually landed a position. Walter, by contrast, fell into a helpless and hopeless outlook. "I got fired because I can't perform under pressure," he thought. "I'm not cut out for finance. The economy will take years to recover." Even as the market improved, he didn't look for another job; he ended up moving back in with his parents.

Seligman summed up the differences in the two experiences: "Douglas and Walter stand at opposite ends of the continuum of reactions to failure. The Douglases of the world bounce back after a brief period of malaise; within a year they've grown because of the experience. The Walters go from sadness to depression to a paralyzing fear of the future. Yet failure is a nearly inevitable part of work, and it is one of life's most common traumas."

Seligman's work with the U.S. Army has gleaned valuable insights into how to recover from failure in general. "On one end are the people who fall apart into PTSD, depression, and even suicide. In the middle are most people, who at first react with symptoms of depression and anxiety but within a month or so are, by physical and psychological measures, back where they were before the trauma. That is resilience. On the other end are people who show post-traumatic growth. They, too, first experience depression and anxiety, often exhibiting full-blown PTSD; but within a year they are better off than they were before the trauma," wrote Seligman.

What propels people to post-traumatic growth? A team led by University of Michigan professor Christopher Peterson, author of the VIA Strengths Survey, worked with Seligman on the Army project. More than 900,000 soldiers have taken the VIA Survey. The resulting database has enabled positive psychologists to answer questions like: What specific character strengths protect against PTSD, depression, and anxiety? Does a strong sense of meaning result in better performance? Are people who score high in positive emotion promoted more quickly? Can optimism spread from a leader to followers? Said Seligman, "We believe that business people can draw lessons from this approach, particularly in times of failure and stagnation. Working with both individual soldiers (employees) and drill sergeants (managers), we are helping to create an army of Douglases who can turn their most difficult experiences into catalysts for improved performance."

Babe Ruth once held the record for the most home runs. Did you know he also held the record for the most strikeouts? Get the connection? You might fail time and again, but if you keep swinging the bat, you take a chance that you might eclipse those failures with successes.

It is undeniable that post-traumatic growth corresponds with character strengths:

- Improved relationships (kindness, love)
- Openness to new possibilities (curiosity, creativity, learning)
- Appreciation of life (appreciation of beauty, gratitude, zest)
- Personal strength (bravery, honesty, perseverance)
- Spiritual development (spirituality)[6]

Sometimes experiences you perceive as failures are opportunities that signal that your ego is in the driver's seat rather than your authentic self. Our failures can be the turning points in our lives, revealing what our true purpose is. But you have to be willing to look at the message of the failure and put it in the context of your long-term goals and values.[5]

Coaching Tip

Dealing with past failures or painful experiences can be challenging. Coaching is not about getting mired in the past. It is about creating a new and better future. Notice that the questions in this area help the person being coached to think about the future in a hopeful and optimistic manner. Psychologists and psychiatrists are well-trained to explore deep-seated mental and emotional issues, so seek help if you encounter challenges beyond coaching.

STRONG Questions©: Reframe Failure

✓ Which strengths and strengths combinations could I best apply to this situation?

✓ If this situation were custom-designed to stretch and grow me, how would that change my perspective?

✓ What would I do if I believed in my strengths and myself?

✓ If I could change my perception, what would change?

✓ What's the best possible outcome for this situation?

✓ How have I successfully addressed similar situations/patterns in my life? How could I recreate success?

✓ What benefits would result by letting go of grudges?

While the motivational power of
self-criticism comes from fear
of self-punishment, the
motivational power of

SELF-COMPASSION

comes from the
desire to be your best.

Dr. Kristin Neff

8 | MINDFUL EMOTIONS

"To merge character strengths and mindfulness is to bring a deep awareness to our best qualities and to use these qualities to improve our awareness of all aspects of our lives. Mindfulness and character strengths deepen one another. To practice using character strengths with mindfulness is to be intentional and conscious about noticing and deploying your best qualities."

—*Dr. Ryan M. Niemiec*

When guiding people to more effectively manage their negative emotions, I coach them that instead of running from a difficult situation, they will likely get better results by "connecting" to the emotion—in other words, accepting reality in that moment. Without judging, condemning, criticizing, shaming, or rejecting what has presented itself. They must simply be willing to experience an unavoidable situation and their feelings rather than falling into denial, lashing out, or resisting the sometimes painful moment. Being mindful leads to truthful, authentic living and ultimately enables us to transform our negative emotions while creating a better future. The key is to learn a way to experience and express our feelings that serves us without damaging our relationships.

Embracing a negative situation does not mean you don't prefer, hope for, or work toward something better. It is not a passive approach to life—being tossed about by whatever the winds blow your way. For example, in psychology classes, mindfulness students learn to experience the moment as it is; but that does not mean they do not have preferences. Most people who practice mindfulness would much prefer the world to be much less contentious and far more compassionate. Yet the very act of being mindful allows us to embrace hard moments when life presents situations riddled with conflict, stress or failure, and subsequently to learn and grow from these experiences.

Developing mindfulness serves us well not only in a personal context but also professionally. Mindfulness has been shown to increase focus and productivity, while multitasking has been shown to lower overall productivity. Research reveals that students and workers who constantly and rapidly switch between tasks have less ability to filter out irrelevant information, and they make more mistakes. A 2013 GFI Software report shows that eighty-one percent of U.S. employees check their work email outside of work hours and read email during weddings, funerals, and other family events. In a performance environment, mindfulness produces a more desirable outcome.

Connect

A monk once taught the following equation: Pain x Resistance = Suffering.[2] The more we resist negative emotions by assaulting ourselves with all the "should haves," "could haves," and "would haves" in a situation, the more we suffer. Does this self-talk sound familiar? "I should have known better." "If only I had the resources, I could have made a better choice." "I would have done that differently if she hadn't pushed my buttons." We all have painful negative emotions—and resisting them only heightens their damaging effect. Emotions often are experienced like a wave; they can build and crest. But if we are mindful, they typically don't stay at their height and eventually flow back to normal. If they are stuffed (like damming a river), they can become stagnant and toxic—and the emotion levels, like water levels behind a dam, can remain high as a result.

This practice of connecting to and objectively observing our negative emotions enables us to process the negative emotions rather than fighting, fleeing from, or stuffing them. Learning to properly process negative emotions deflates much of the power they exert. Practicing mindfulness in this way—"connecting" to the present reality—develops emotional intelligence because we are cultivating a deeper awareness of ourselves and our emotions and learning to better self-regulate. This healthy approach allows us to strengthen our relationship with ourselves and others, ultimately making us more productive and content.

Authentic vs. Debilitating Negative Emotions

Negative emotions are part of life. Some are authentic and necessary for growth, and some are counterfeit and debilitating. Understanding which type of negativity we are experiencing determines which tools we can use to return to a positive emotional state. Authentic negative emotions spark growth. Positive psychology has uncovered that some negativity grounds us in reality and that embracing the painful truth encourages us to learn and grow in our lives. For example, it is natural to mourn the loss of someone dear to you, to feel guilt when you do something you know is wrong, to be angry when you see an injustice, or disappointed when something you really want eludes you. At times, fully experiencing relationships and life in general requires us to feel negative emotions. The research reveals that if we suppress these negative feelings, they inevitably grow stronger and surface in other parts of our lives. We will learn later in this chapter how to acknowledge and experience these authentic negative emotions in a healthy way.

By contrast, debilitating negative emotions cause useless stress and suffering. As if life's innate challenges are not enough, we often multiply the negative emotions we feel by becoming our own worst critic throughout the painful experience. For example, on top of the authentic disappointment when we fail to land the dream job, we sometimes add the following self-criticisms: "I'm not smart enough." "I never measure up." "Nothing ever seems to work out for me." "I'm a loser." "I'll never get a job, and I'll live in my parents' basement forever." Recognize some of these? The part of our brains that is wired for survival in a hostile world kicks in. We tend to over-generalize and catastrophize the event and may even lapse into viewing ourselves as a victim.

The Buddhist teaching of the Two Arrows helps us better understand authentic vs. debilitating negative emotions.[3] When afflicted with a negative emotion, we often feel deep sorrow and grief. The larger problem is that afterward we sometimes also fall prey to ruminating, becoming distraught or bitter, or falling into despair. So we feel two pains. It is just like being shot with an arrow, and right afterwards being shot with a second and more debilitating one. Thus we can see the distinction between pain on the one hand and our self-imposed suffering from pain on the other. How we experience pain can agonize and debilitate us, like the second and even more lethal arrow.

In our instant gratification culture, perceiving this distinction between the two arrows has become blurred because as soon as we feel discomfort, we tend to reach for some external fix (food, self-medication, distraction) to alleviate the discomfort. There are many ways that we avoid reality in the moment. These may include denying, rationalizing, explaining away our situation, or trying to push our feelings into the background. We may try to handle our pain by projecting our anger onto others, getting lost in self-pity, torturing ourselves with guilt, and so on. Once we become familiar with our evasions, we can become more intimate with the deeper feelings we seek to evade—like fear, despair, anger and shame. To acknowledge these painful emotions requires courage and determination, but it is the first step to transforming them. Transformation occurs after we first embrace our situation as it is.

The practice of mindfulness can enable us to experience our negative emotions so they feel less acute and more manageable. And more, it can enable us to work with our afflictions so that we begin to experience the whole of life in a more productive way.

When dealing with negative emotions, the STRONG Filter© approach has proven effective for many. The next time you feel negative emotions, step one is to distinguish between the authentic negative emotions that produce growth when worked through and the debilitating negative emotions that produce only discouragement, despair, and disengagement. Note the characteristics of each below:

Authentic Emotions

- Encourage authenticity, positive change, and growth
- Are based on reasonable expectations, objective facts and truth
- Increase confidence

Debilitating Emotions

- Discourage authenticity, produce despair/disengagement
- Are based on unreasonable expectations, distorted facts, self-deception
- Decrease confidence

The next step is to ask yourself: "What am I feeling that is based on unreasonable or irrational expectations?" "What am I feeling that is based on objective facts and truth?" Many people find that just applying this "authentic" vs. "debilitating" emotions filter can help them sift through life's most challenging moments.

Connecting to Emotions

I had a coaching conversation with a talented teacher and writer who shared a breakthrough experience she had in dealing with recurring negative emotions. She had accompanied her socially astute teenage daughter on a performing tour. Her adolescent memories of being the lonely outcast resurfaced when several of the chaperones on the trip turned out to be a tight-knit group who had known each other for years. Exacerbating her insecurity was her desire for her daughter to feel proud of her. Throughout the entire trip, she felt like she just didn't fit in as she repeatedly failed to break into the group. "It felt just like high school all over again," she told me later.

On the plane ride home, she was seated next to one of the moms she had tried to befriend. "At last, a chance to connect," she thought. At that exact moment, the woman excused herself and moved up to an empty seat in the midst of a group of moms several rows ahead.

Left alone in a row, she struggled in vain not to take it personally and buried herself in her book. As she listened to the three women laugh and share stories, she physically felt her heart start to close up and harden defensively.

She noticed her thoughts drifting into self pity and a downward spiral, remembering other painful, lonely times..."I just feel so lonely," she thought. Instead of giving voice to the inner critic, she asked for comfort.

The answer that came to her: "Just let yourself feel your loneliness; you don't need to think any more lonely thoughts." She felt the piercing ache of exclusion, followed by compassion for herself, which gradually transformed into a glowing fire of love and brightness, and filled her with a peaceful warmth and joy.

After savoring the feeling, she felt a confidence inspiring her to join the group and was immediately welcomed into the conversation. Relating the story, she said, "I didn't stuff my emotions like I had many times before. I allowed myself to feel their full depth, and I experienced resolution. I had mourned, and I was comforted."

This time she did not run away from what she was feeling, drowning the discomfort in distraction. She challenged herself to be present in the moment, to face her fear of exclusion, allowing herself to experience it so that she could ultimately transcend it. By doing so, she made it past her insecurity and overcame a pattern of thinking that had held her hostage for years.

Self Care

After we have allowed ourselves to connect and experience our negative emotion(s), it is vital to offer ourselves self-care. A helpful technique you can use is practicing the art of self-compassion. Positive psychologists Kristin Neff's and Christopher Germer's research in the field of self-compassion is showing that the healthy way to manage unavoidable negative emotions is to fully feel them while practicing self-soothing techniques, and soon your negative emotions will soften and eventually lose their powerful, debilitating grip.

> When we deal honestly with our emotions, we can extend compassion to ourselves.

When we deal honestly with our emotions, we can extend genuine compassion to ourselves. This enables us to feel cared for, accepted, and secure. The heaviness of negative emotions is offset by our self-care. We are then able to shift our focus to our character strengths and employ them in finding effective solutions. The self-produced feelings of well-being and safety then deactivate the body's threat system, calming down the amygdala and stress chemicals being released, thereby increasing the production of positive chemicals released by the brain.[4]

Neff identifies three key elements of self-compassion. The first is self-kindness, which entails being kind and understanding toward ourselves when we suffer, fail, or feel inadequate, rather than ignoring our pain or flagellating ourselves with self-criticism. The second is common humanity. The frustration we experience at not having things exactly as we want is often accompanied by an irrational sense of isolation—as if we are the only person suffering or making mistakes. And the third is mindfulness. Self-compassion requires taking a balanced, mindful approach to our negative emotions so that our feelings are neither suppressed nor exaggerated.[5]

The Undoing Effect

The next step in "undoing" a negative emotion is to intentionally cultivate positive emotions to take its place. Have you ever been overcome by a negative emotion only to be surprised at how quickly your negative emotion dissipates when a positive emotion becomes the new focus? Maybe it was an unexpected phone call from a loved one, an inspiring quote you stumbled across, your favorite song playing on the radio, something on TV that made you smile? How did that happen? What if you could learn to "undo" negative emotions when needed?

Evidence for the "undoing effect" of positive emotions suggests that people can improve their psychological well-being, and perhaps also their physical health, by cultivating experiences of positive emotions at opportune moments to cope with negative emotions. A positive emotion may loosen the hold that a negative emotion has gained on a person's mind and body.[6] Scientists tested this undoing effect by first inducing a negative emotion in all participants by assigning a time-pressured speech. In just one minute, participants had to prepare a speech. They were led to believe that their speech would be videotaped and evaluated by their peers. This speech task induced anxiety along with increases in heart rate, peripheral vasoconstriction, and systolic and diastolic blood pressure. Then the scientists randomly assigned participants to view one of four films. Two films elicited mild positive emotions (joy and contentment), a third served as a neutral control condition and a fourth elicited sadness. In three independent samples, participants who watched the two positive emotion films exhibited faster cardiovascular recovery than did those in the neutral control condition. Participants in the sadness condition exhibited the most delayed recovery.[7]

Connect, Care, Create© Tool

I have synthesized what I have found to be the best techniques to manage negative emotions into what I call the "Connect, Care, Create© Tool." This tool helps you work through unavoidable negative emotions associated with personal and professional disappointments, losses or failures. First, because your brain tends to exaggerate a single event and get stuck in an endless cycle of rumination, this process anchors your focus on your body, which helps stop the cycle by giving your brain something new to focus on. Second, it prompts you toward self-care and helps you accept that negative emotions are a part of life. Third, this process helps you learn how to transform a negative emotion by using your strengths as a lens to address the issue, thus creating new positive emotions to undo the effect of the negative emotion. In practicing this tool, people tell me there is a sense of relief, liberation, and a freedom from rumination that opens them to real growth. The most encouraging part of this approach is that we can learn to productively process negative emotions.[8] After all, you are the one person in your life that is always around when you are feeling negative emotions, so why not learn to deliver the best antidote?

Connect	Get in a comfortable seated position. Become mindful of and connect to the negative emotion you are feeling. Embrace all aspects of the emotion without judging it, shaming it, avoiding it or running from it. Just let yourself experience it truthfully and objectively. If you contributed to the situation, acknowledge your role honestly using self compassion rather than self-criticism. Where in your body do you feel the emotion most?

Care	Practice self-care. Relax the area where you are holding the negative emotion (your stomach, shoulders, chest, back, etc.) and imagine it dissolving like an ice cube in warm water. Send yourself compassion, reminding yourself that everyone experiences difficult moments, loss, mistakes, and failure. Reassure yourself that you will give yourself the support you need to get through this experience and that you will take steps to better the situation.
Create	What strength(s) can you call forward to help you transform this negative emotion and create a positive outcome? How can you learn and grow from this experience? What new positive emotions are you feeling now...hope, forgiveness, love, perspective, kindness, self-regulation? Notice as your negative emotion gradually dissipates and loses its power over you, and as new, positive emotions are created in its place.

Disclaimer: Some negative emotions, like those rooted in mental health issues, substance abuse, abusive environments, etc., may require the help of a medical professional or therapist. Please seek appropriate help.

Connect, Care, Create© in Action

A great example of activating the principles of "connect, care, create" is Mother Teresa. One day Mother Teresa went to a local bakery to ask for bread for the hungry children in the orphanage. The baker, outraged at people begging for bread from him, spat in her face and refused. Mother Teresa calmly took out her handkerchief, wiped the spit from her face and said to the baker, "Thank you. That was for me. Now, what about the bread for the orphans?" The baker was so moved by her reaction that he became a consistent donor.[9]

What I love about this story, aside from the strengths of courage, forgiveness, perseverance, self-regulation, humility, and love demonstrated by Mother Teresa, is how she manages to peacefully change the baker's mind and emotional response. Mother Teresa shows us how to react to insult without being a doormat, how to experience and persevere through a negative situation and transform it through emotional self-regulation. She didn't fight, flee or stuff her emotions, but instead connected to the reality of the moment. She knew that if she had not taken the insulting spit in full grace, the children at the orphanage would have gone on being hungry. She was being guided by her purpose, and her devotion to that purpose was sufficient to weather the storms of offense, providing a positive emotion to undo the negative emotion: dignity in the midst of disrespect.

Coaching Tip

Hone your self-awareness. Resolve to use the authentic vs. debilitating filter that you learned about on the previous pages when you experience negative emotions.

STRONG Questions©: Mindful Emotions

- ✓ What am I feeling that is based on objective facts and truth?
- ✓ What am I feeling that is based on unreasonable or irrational expectations?
- ✓ How am I resisting and prolonging the effects of the present reality?
- ✓ How can I best observe the emotion(s) to better understand it and its source?
- ✓ How can I reassure myself that I will give myself the support I need to get through this difficult time?
- ✓ What character strengths can best help me in this situation?
- ✓ What resources can I access to best comfort and support myself through this?
- ✓ What aspect of this challenging situation and emotion(s) will help me to learn and grow most?
- ✓ What about this emotion(s) helps me to better empathize with others?
- ✓ How can this experience best serve me going forward?

Part | ENGAGE YOUR
III | STRENGTHS

"Your greatest self has been waiting your whole life; don't make it wait any longer."

—Dr. Steve Maraboli

"The third stage of the ASA Coaching Process is called 'Engage.' This stage is literally strengths in action. It is where the rubber meets the road, and we now take our carefully designed goals and act on them. We engage our strengths by deploying them regularly, building them through targeted activities and using the weekly 3 R's© process which is based on the principle of positive progression—all the while honoring the strengths in others."

—Fatima Doman

All learning
has an
EMOTIONAL
base.

Plato

9 | CHARACTER STRENGTHS FUEL EMOTIONAL INTELLIGENCE

"I've learned that people will forget what you said, people will forget what you did, but people will never forget how you made them feel."

—*Maya Angelou*

"Emotional intelligence skills are synergistic with cognitive ones; top performers have both. The more complex the job, the more emotional intelligence matters—if only because a deficiency in these abilities can hinder the use of whatever technical expertise or intellect a person may have."

—*Dr. Daniel Goleman*

Trudy never got to stand up at a middle school or high school assembly as the parent of a high achiever. Sometimes it seemed like every other parent in the school had stood up to accept some kind of applause for their child's accomplishments but her. Her son was of average intelligence and tried his best, although he had a learning disability in reading and writing.

Several years after her son had graduated from high school, he had become a surprisingly good student at a technical college. One day, Trudy was talking to a friend who was a teacher at her son's high school. The teacher asked if her son's name was Robert. The teacher said when she asked another teacher friend at her retirement party who her favorite student had been, she named Robert, Trudy's son.

Trudy was stunned. "You must be mistaken," she said. "My son never distinguished himself in high school."

The reason the retiring English teacher had remembered him, even though English was likely his worst subject, was that "he was such a fine young man—so thoughtful, and such a positive attitude." Trudy had heard similar things during school conferences; several teachers had said something to the effect that although her son did not excel in his schoolwork, he was so honest and personable that they felt sure he would do well. She had a hard time believing that—anxious that her son wasn't getting better grades or setting higher goals.

But he did get good grades after graduation from high school and went on to a career in the health field. He excelled at every job he took on his way to a permanent position as a respiratory therapist at the Veterans Administration Hospital, where he not only saved lives but trained others in bedside manner. In addition, he was a dedicated volunteer firefighter and paramedic in his community. Ten years out of high school, he was married, owned a home, was an active member of his church and community, had a good income, and had great job security.

Although Trudy's sons's IQ and other test scores had always been low, anecdotal evidence and his present successes indicate he has many highly developed character strengths, which translates into a high EQ—or emotional intelligence—a characteristic he shares with many senior level executives.

Emotional Intelligence in the 21st. Century

In his book, *Humans are Underrated: What High Achievers Know That Brilliant Machines Never Will*, Fortune's Geoff Colvin explains that people will always insist on some jobs being done by human beings even if computers are capable of doing those jobs. These jobs that draw upon emotional intelligence are going to be the jobs of the future because humans are social animals. Colvin calls those who excel at working with others "relationship workers," and predicts they will be the most valuable workers of the twenty-first century. The jobs of the future will require social and emotional intelligence fueled by character.

For the purposes of this book, an extremely simplified definition of emotional intelligence (EQ) is: the capacity for recognizing our own feelings and those of others, and the ability to manage those feelings to motivate ourselves and others to do their best. For further information on the topic, I highly recommend Dr. Daniel Goleman's groundbreaking work on EQ, and his book, *Emotional Intelligence at Work*. Dr. Goleman, as the world's leading authority on emotional intelligence, presented the proposition in the mid-1990s that being "book smart," or having high IQ scores, or even graduating from Ivy League schools does not guarantee success. And guess what? Many character strengths make up emotional intelligence, such as prudence, self-regulation, social intelligence, and teamwork, just to mention a few.

What is so compelling about EQ? Why has the mainstream marketplace been inundated by this concept—a concept that was originally the province of academic research on intelligences and capabilities? I spent a week taking a course from Goleman and his wife, Tara, and during that week discussed that question and more over meals with him. He told me this concept of coaching is so exciting to him because it focuses on bringing to the surface the strengths in people and helping them understand when and where they can best apply their strengths to create their best future.

Character Strengths Fuel Emotional Intelligence

In my coaching, I talk with my clients about building character strengths intelligence—what I call CSQ. I believe character strengths intelligence (CSQ) fuels emotional intelligence (EQ). Many mistakenly view CSQ or EQ as something you either have or you don't—like charisma or a high IQ. Not true. First of all, CSQ and EQ, unlike IQ, can be learned and enhanced. Research shows that CSQ and EQ are often more important than IQ in almost every role—but especially in leadership roles.

Goleman's model represents four competency clusters for emotional intelligence: two under the category of personal competence and two under social competence. His model aligns perfectly with the personal and social awareness that comes from understanding our strengths. In many ways, understanding and applying character strengths (CSQ) is synonymous with emotional intelligence (EQ) competencies and actually fuels emotional intelligence.

153

Emotional Intelligence:

> **Personal Competence:** This competency cluster includes self-awareness and self-management. Self-awareness is the ability to recognize a feeling as it is happening, to identify what it is, where it is coming from, and why. It is useful because it allows us to understand what we're doing well, what motivates us, and what we don't handle well—triggers. Self-management is the ability to use the awareness of your emotions to manage your behavior, being the calm port in a storm.

> **Social Competence:** This competency cluster includes social awareness and relationship management. Social awareness is being able to pick up on other people's emotions then listen, observe, and empathize. Relationship management is the ability to build solid relationships through communication and to handle conflict in a productive rather than punitive way.[1] (Goleman, 2005).

Developing your intrapersonal and interpersonal strengths through "consistent practices" fuels emotional intelligence. Many change agents believe it takes on average from twenty-one to thirty days to form a new, consistent behavior; so the key is to work on forming one new emotionally intelligent, strengths-based "practice" at a time, experiencing progressive success, then focusing on the next one you want to form.

Transparency and Accountability

Aristotle challenged humanity to manage its emotional and intellectual life with character. We have long since struggled with that call to develop character as a society as evidenced by the media's exposure of corrupted companies. It is more important than ever that leaders exhibit strengths of character and promote a policy of corporate transparency and social responsibility that will restore the public's trust in our government, educational institutions, and corporations.

The tide is changing. Greedy and aggressive behavior and poor customer service are quickly exposed these days. A company's reputation can be devastated in a concerted, grass roots social networking campaign. Mature, balanced, transparent, emotionally competent, and character-driven behavior is expected.

By far the most inspiring leader I've ever experienced was my boss, Paula, who was very much an individual guided by her character strengths. When I first met her, I mentioned to her a presentation I was putting together. My industry was competitive, and it was important to have something unique and cutting edge in my presentation. I asked her for only one particular slide, knowing that she had developed her own distinct presentations through years of work. She took me into her office and opened up two file cabinets and said, "Fatima, take anything you like," and left me alone in her office.

I felt like I had stumbled on a bonanza of not only helpful information for my presentation, but of generosity, teamwork, leadership, and complete transparency. Her openness demonstrated her confidence in herself and her belief in me. Throughout the years she rose to executive vice president level, lifting up the people around her and publicly praising people who reported to her. Her teams thrived.

Another experience I had witnessing emotional intelligence fueled by character strengths was while consulting for a company executive. I presented an idea that was important to me, but took us all off track at his team meeting. Roger gracefully got us back on track without invalidating or devaluing my idea so I could remain confident about contributing in the future. He could have squelched my enthusiasm, but he had trained himself over time to put important relationships first, rather than letting a meeting agenda lead him into frustration. He was able to express that he was glad I had shared an important idea that should be captured for future discussion, but that we needed to get back to where we were. There was no chastising, just a very genuine thank you and a commitment to follow up. He exercised his strengths of social intelligence, teamwork, and kindness by choosing to focus on the relationship rather than on the need to accomplish something immediately, at the expense of morale.

A great leader doesn't want to be the only leader.

Successful corporations are no longer autocracies. A great leader doesn't want to be the only leader. It takes input and feedback to create a compelling vision. Today's successful organizations are learning that encouraging more people to lead is where the edge is. Our organizations are counting on us to bring our unique character strengths to work so we can combine them with the strengths of others to build a better whole. The proverbial nodding "yes" man or woman does no one any good.

Strengths Authenticity: CSQ

When we are living inauthentic lives, unable to express our unique character strengths, we lose our connection to ourselves and little by little can develop self-directed frustration, anger, and mistrust that extend to others. The antidote to that is to practice strengths authenticity, which becomes a natural calling card in the world via our character. Developing awareness and appreciation of our strengths as well as those of others, while making a conscious effort to deploy everyone's strengths where appropriate, is the key. Conversely, trying to force people to fit into roles that are not authentic for them over the long-term can deflate a project and a team. In fact, there are

> A wonderful thing about emotional intelligence is that it grows through optimal use of our character strengths.

positive psychology studies indicating that heart patients have damaged their hearts by faking smiles and positive attitudes, similar to the ventricle constriction that can be observed when people experience intensely negative emotions.[2] If the positivity is not authentic, then you need to develop self-awareness in order to explore ways to reframe a negative state into a positive one, genuinely. In fact, new research shows that insincere positivity can be as corrosive as anger. Even for the happiest people, denying hard times doesn't make them go away. I've never subscribed to the adage, "Fake it till you make it." I prefer to tell my clients, "Embrace it to transform it." I have discovered that when people connect to their authentic signature strengths, they find that added measure of energy needed to transform challenging situations.

A wonderful thing about emotional intelligence is that it grows through the optimal use of our character strengths and, although it often develops naturally with age, it can also grow when one practices authenticity. It's not about learning a script. It is about developing a new perception of reality centered on being a contribution to others. What is the cost to the organization's creativity if ideas are discounted or if team members are silenced or shamed? What might be lost due to impatience and lack of tact? The key, as we learned earlier, is to approach these moments as a strengths coach rather than as a critic.

Embracing Change

It is our human, not superhuman, attributes that make great leaders.[3] Those human attributes include the capacity to cooperate, to co-create, and also to change both our social capital and ourselves.

Adaptability is essential in both the business world and in the social world of relationships. The marketplace changes, but so do our needs as we go through the stages of our lives. An endorsement for the VIA Strengths Inventory reads, "Leaders who excel at interpersonal courage often form authentic relationships with their colleagues—the kind of relationships that generate deep emotional commitment to both individuals and the company. Enduring personal change originates within each individual." I have noticed a ripple effect with my coaching clients who lead authentically from their character strengths—their behavior is passed on through personal and professional relationships to larger communities.

People too often view their need to change as a sign of failure or weakness. In fact, change opens the door to the freedom to experiment and innovate, and often leads to better ideas, products, and successes. As Alexander Pope said, "A man should never be ashamed to own he has been in the wrong, which is but saying, in other words, that he is wiser today than he was yesterday."[4]

Coaching Tip

Give your CSQ (Character Strength Intelligence) and EQ (Emotional Intelligence) a good workout by asking the following questions designed to explore self-awareness/ management and social awareness/relationship management.

STRONG Questions©: CSQ

✓ How can I develop a better awareness of my strengths?

✓ Which of my intrapersonal strengths can I use to develop my self-awareness? (See VIA Two Factor Graph)

✓ Which of my interpersonal strengths can I use to develop my social awareness? (See VIA Two Factor Graph)

✓ What can I do to better understand my feelings/emotions and better manage expressing them?

✓ What strengths can I use to enhance my ability to listen to and better understand others?

✓ What differences of strengths do I value in others, and how are they beneficial?

✓ How can I help myself and others view humility as a strength rather than a weakness?

✓ How can I better hone my strengths of social intelligence, leadership, and teamwork?

✓ What is an important personal relationship I would like to develop? A professional relationship I would like to develop? How will I do this?

Positive institutions not only elevate and connect human strengths, but also serve to refract and magnify our highest human strengths into SOCIETY

Dr. David Cooperrider

10 | THE SMART SWARM

"With a moment's reflection it becomes clear: positive emotions foster the very kinds of skills corporations want in their leadership teams and that our coaching clients would like to build in themselves."

—Dr. Carol Kauffman

Gary, a CEO, had deployed his right-hand man, Frank, on a new project that was entrepreneurial in nature and different from other undertakings they had worked on together previously. Frank's assignment was to figure out ways to distribute a new product the company had produced. It required setting up new distribution channels and partners the company had not used before.

Gary became frustrated with how slowly things were progressing, and Frank was becoming frustrated with Gary's disappointment. The two developed tension in what otherwise had always been a good working relationship. Gary decided to sit down with Frank and go over each other's VIA results.

They discussed how Gary's top character strengths were creativity and perseverance, which led him to just go out and try new things and keep persisting until he succeeded. Frank's top character strengths were judgment and prudence, which made him want to do things only after they had been thought through thoroughly and seemed to have a high likelihood of success. This discussion helped Gary realize that Frank's strengths were complementary to his own, and that is why they had always been such a good team. Learning each other's strengths caused Gary to appreciate that Frank's approach, though different from his, could work as well. Once Gary had acknowledged this about Frank, he let him do the project by leading with his own strengths. The project was a huge success.

In this chapter I will offer you a new perspective on both yourself and those with whom you interact, resulting in new possibilities for improving your success and fulfillment in life. We will explore what VIA calls the "dance" that goes on between people on teams and in organizations. Sometimes that dance can be clumsy and downright painful when someone steps on our toes. Other times it is poetry to behold. How do we develop the ability to dance fluidly with a variety of people in ever-changing circumstances? Like Frank and Gary came to see, recognizing and appreciating one another's strengths is the key.

Many people feel like they are mismatched in their jobs and with their coworkers and find themselves in a "crisis of disengagement." In fact, eighty percent of respondents in a Gallup Global Workforce study were found to be "not flourishing."

We certainly can't expect our organizations to run well if we don't achieve a good fit between the employees and what they are doing. The question becomes, how do leaders ensure a good fit for their employees, and how do employees assess how they best fit in their team and in their organization? A *Harvard Business Review* report showed that engagement significantly increases performance.[1] Therefore, it's in everyone's best interest to find our best fit with what we do and with the people with whom we work.

In 2012 *Harvard Business Review* devoted an entire issue to this topic, elaborating on the summary statement on its cover—"How Employee Well-Being Drives Profits." A study by Killingworth in 2012 reported, "Happiness on the job may depend more on our moment-to-moment experiences than on conditions such as a high salary or a prestigious title."[2] These findings can be useful in both the work setting and in our personal lives to help us better understand what motivates us and others.

Psychologically speaking, we all come in different sizes and shapes. We all have different strengths profiles. The key is to bring ourselves into focus—to find our "strengths fingerprint"—and then to figure out how to put our "fingerprint" on our work.[3] The VIA Survey helps us define our unique strengths so we can then find our best place to connect.

> **The key is to bring ourselves into focus — find our "strengths fingerprint" — and then figure out how to put our "fingerprint" on our work.**

To operate a company as if people are machine parts engineered to perform functions without proper recognition of their humanity is a dire mistake. When companies operate with recognition of the humanity of their labor force, they unleash human potential, *e.g.*, creativity, adjustments, increased output, etc.[4] Character strengths (especially signature strengths) are the most important aspect of ourselves that we want recognized and understood by others and that are important for us to express. Virtually every company's annual report claims that its people are its biggest asset, yet research shows that only a miniscule number of organizations manage employees in such a way that they feel valued and appreciated for their strengths.

Strengths Transform Work Into a Calling

When we find a way to put our fingerprint on our work, our work then becomes a calling, in that it calls forth what is best in us: our character strengths. We not only want to do things we can do well, we want to do things we *care* about doing well. An excellent example of this is the famous doctor, Albert Schweitzer, awarded the Nobel Peace Price in 1953. His expression "reverence for life" permeated his life's work. He shared with the world his firm belief that no person must ever harm or destroy life unless

> **We not only want to do things we can do well, we want to do things we *care* about doing well.**

absolutely necessary. He wanted to alleviate suffering, so together with his wife, who was a nurse, he built and ran a hospital in Gabon, a French colony at the time. This effort became an example to others.[5]

In order to become engaged in our work and to find fulfillment, we can look to find personal expression in what we do and insert our whole selves into our work. We not only want to do things that allow us to feel competent and able to compete (talents), we want to also do things that make us feel satisfied and complete (character strengths).

A company, after doing all it can in its recruitment and staff development efforts, has X amount of talent on board—and its challenge is to get the most out of that talent. The way for companies to do this is to energize and enliven their workforce through the recognition and deployment of character strengths. This is what can take a company from good to great. As Dr. Mayerson points out, "Character strengths are the fuel and the rudder. If our talents are not directed well and energized well, we underperform."[6]

The Smart Swarm

Often, things in nature that appear to be disorganized on the surface are actually behaving in a much more intelligent way that may not be obvious. This is called "self-organizing." Dynamic teams do not always function in simple linear fashion, but rather like a swarm of birds or insects. Optimum functioning groups distribute important knowledge among their members as opposed to having it reside in just a few. Diversity of character strength profiles allows for a diversity of perspectives and insights that should be nurtured and utilized, as opposed to discouraged and punished.

A high functioning team is like a smart swarm, understanding that the collective actions of the group will be smarter if communication networks are rich and open. The group benefits from bringing together the different pieces of information that are spread throughout many people. Consider the TV show "Who Wants to Be a Millionaire?" It's been said that when a contestant opts to "phone a friend," that friend (an expert) is right only sixty-five percent of the time, while the audience is right ninety-one percent of the time. Our collective wisdom and knowledge is greater than that residing in a select few "leaders" or "experts."

Self-organizing has its own innate intelligence. Studies of high performing organizations show that they are characterized by these rich inter-communications—which demonstrates that it is wise to respect the wisdom that resides in an organization's distributed knowledge. To better align our character strengths with our work, we can look to three points of connection. One point of connection or alignment is to the organization's mission and values. How can you best bring your signature strengths to serve that mission?

A second point of connection or alignment is with particular functions and tasks that you perform in service of the organization's mission. Team functions are activities that successful teams tend to engage in. VIA has defined what they call the "7 Team Functions" common to teams, and a panel of business experts and positive psychologists have mapped the VIA character strengths with these various functions. They are ideas, information gathering, decision making, implementation, influencing, relationship management, and energy management.

And finally, a third point of connection is found through learning the "team dance," the give and take within teams. Just as an example, a swarm of birds may have only two simple rules: follow your immediate neighbors, and don't bump into anyone. Smart teams also tend to have just a few simple rules, and connecting involves figuring out what those few rules are and following them.

Stepping Up and Making Room

Once you understand that a team is not about others lining up behind you and you lining up behind others, the ebb and flow of the team, involving give and take, will work better. There are any number of places where you can make your alignment and connection. Another important concept is to understand where you can contribute or "step up." And then we need to know when to "make room" for others when they have something to contribute. For example, teams that function well have everyone involved—at some times in roles of talking or leading a discussion, and at other times in roles of listening or asking probing questions.

The dance is a process of fluidly moving between stepping up and making room. Each team develops a dance where the person in the lead changes as the work unfolds. High performing teams are characterized by everybody participating, with each person understanding what he can deliver in service of the team.

Turn Collisions into Collaboration

Sometimes, the dance gets out of rhythm and we start clumsily bumping into each other. One person's strength may collide with another's strength. That's when we need to learn not to step on each other's toes. Let's say one of my signature strengths is "love of learning." I may assume that everyone loves learning as much as I do and drone on in conversations, *ad infinitum*. I might lose sight of the fact that my team member is biting her nails. She will interject, and I'll feel that she's cutting me off, and I'll be offended. This misunderstanding can be avoided if we understand our differences and recognize one another's strengths at the onset, developing awareness about how we can come together as a team and collaborate.

Since all character strengths are positive, we don't have to be embarrassed about any of our strengths. But we do have to learn to appreciate one another's character strengths.[7] It's like a good potluck meal—which takes everyone bringing something different to the meal to make it successful.

Take Back Your Remote Control© Tool

Strengths collisions are not uncommon in work environments. I use the following three-step "Take Back Your Remote Control"© Tool to help people who want to gain better control over their automatic reactions. Thoughtfully address the following three steps and take back your remote control!

Step 1: Recall	Recall a situation where you consistently get your buttons pushed and tend to respond from a "critic" mindset (e.g., impatience, passive/aggressive behaviors, lack of self-discipline).
Step 2: Identify	Identify strengths being expressed by the other person and why their strengths may be colliding with yours. Consider how appreciating one another's strengths might improve the situation. Identify one or two of your strengths that you could use to respond more effectively next time. How can you respond in a new way that leverages your strengths and serves you better in the future?
Step 3: List	List the positive outcomes of responding in this new, strengths-focused way, and list who and what would be impacted.

Take Back Your Remote Control, © Authentic Strengths Advantage Coaching, 2014

Team Strengths Culture

The more that individuals on a team make an effort to recognize one another's strengths, the more likely those particular strengths will influence the culture of the team. The team culture will affect the tone and feel of the team and suggest action tendencies. Your team character strengths culture dictates which strengths are most encouraged and which behaviors will be expressed the most enthusiastically. For example, a team in which a majority of members possess curiosity may be most energetic about exploring new ideas and possibilities. On the other hand, a team high in self-regulation and perseverance may get enthused about issues of implementation, meeting deadlines, and staying on budget.

The strengths that the team members have in common can be an important source of cohesion. Yet, these strengths similarities and overlaps can sometimes become areas of conflict when people with similar strengths compete with one another for roles and assignments. Culture can be defined not only by prevalent character strengths, but also by less prevalent or accessible strengths. Certain character strengths may not appear as top strengths in any of a team's members. Simply as a matter of mathematics, smaller teams are more likely than larger ones to have missing signature strengths; and an absence of certain strengths as top strengths could present a challenge to the team. For example, a team without self-regulation or prudence as someone's top strength may have difficulty planning and executing. The solution would be for team members to compensate by calling forward strengths that are middle or lower strengths when the need for that "situational strength" is indicated.

A Culture of Satisfaction

Research has shown that a particular subset of five strengths is most highly related to life satisfaction. These strengths are hope, gratitude, zest, love, and curiosity.[8] These same strengths may be important to work satisfaction to the degree that team members find opportunities for expressing these strengths at work. A team that has one or more of these satisfaction strengths among its cultural strengths likely has a culture of engagement and satisfaction. Given that research shows that positivity is contagious, satisfaction may spread through the team because these particular character strengths are more prevalent in the team culture.

Unique Contributions

When the team knows and honors the unique strengths of each team member, a high functioning team results. While a team member with a love of learning may step forward to report information and facts and lead such a discussion, a team member with perspective may step forward to offer a summary statement that leads the group forward in decision-making. Leadership becomes a dynamic process in which the leader can change moment to moment and situation to situation.

Aligning Team Strengths with Functions

As I stated earlier, every team has a set of functions it performs. Here are seven team functions designed to help you identify how your team's top character strengths may align with particular functions. Try to uncover good fits that may have so far gone unrecognized. On an individual level, explore where your top strengths fit best with the Seven Team Functions and see if, in fact, these are the things you spend most of your time doing at work. You should also consider whether there are team functions that align well with your strengths that you could do more of.

7 Team Functions:

1. **Ideas**: Most efforts begin with the need for generating ideas, and idea generation plays a continuous role through all phases of team functioning. Good ideas are important, and certain strengths are well suited to this function such as creativity, teamwork, bravery, appreciation of beauty and excellence, and especially curiosity.

2. **Information Gathering**: Teams often need to gather information—that is, do homework on topics as varied as potential vendors, competition, best practices, new trends, and so forth. Gathering information is an early and ongoing function that is facilitated by strengths such as love of learning, perseverance, and curiosity.

3. **Decision Making**: Teams need to analyze/process information to arrive at a decision. Analyzing information and arriving at a decision aligns well with strengths such as judgment/critical thinking, perspective, and a good balance of bravery (making bold decisions) and prudence (appropriate caution and good planning).

4. **Implementation**: Once a team has arrived at a decision on its direction, it needs to implement it. A number of strengths can be useful here, including leadership, perseverance, and self-regulation.

5. **Influencing**: Commonly, the work product of the team needs to be presented for acceptance internally (supervisors/administrators) and/or externally (customers). This is a process of influencing and being persuasive. Strengths such as social intelligence, zest, honesty, perspective (seeing the whole picture) and hope can align well with the function of "selling" the final work product to others.

6. **Energy Management**: In the process of getting its work done, teams are helped by having strengths that infuse energy into the work. The team will be energized if there is good alignment of tasks with individuals' strengths. And particular strengths are, in and of themselves, energizing. These include strengths such as zest, hope, love, and humor. Teams without enough energy can fall flat and struggle during times of pressure or prolonged projects that require endurance.

7. **Relationship Management**: Since the working of a team is a dynamic interplay of people and their relationships, strengths that help these relationships run smoothly and resolve conflicts are critically important. These relationship strengths include social intelligence, kindness, fairness, curiosity, and gratitude.

7 Team Functions. (©VIA Institute on Character. All rights reserved. Used with permission.)

The Positive Contagion

Positivity begets more positivity. In fact, research shows that positivity is contagious. When you are positive with another person, he or she is more likely to return the favor. Appreciating others creates an upward spiral of positivity and leads to higher performance. Over 100 research studies conducted globally have shown that when people are exposed to positivity, they see more solutions in puzzles, score higher on cognitive tasks and remember more information. Consider the fact that such an enormous percentage of the workforce felt ignored by their supervisors and were disengaged as a result, according to the previously mentioned Gallup Workforce Study. So the key is to become the catalyst that puts the upward spiral into action. As Dr. Tal Ben-Shahar puts it: "When you appreciate the good, the good appreciates."[9] If each of us is waiting to be appreciated by others, guess what? We will always be waiting to be appreciated by others! What we need to do is begin appreciating others.

Studies show that the most productive work teams are able to communicate respectfully with one another and to create an atmosphere of positivity and openness. Achieving this appreciative atmosphere requires a consciousness of looking for what's going well—again, changing perspective from "what's wrong" to "what's strong"—catching the positives as they occur and not letting them slip by without acknowledgement.[10] Dr. David Cooperrider is at the forefront of new and exciting research that shows that what you focus on literally grows. His work in the field of Appreciative Inquiry is being used to bring about the best in teams around the world. Dr. Cooperrider defines "positive organizations" as having developed the ability to:

1. Consistently see and engage human strengths.

2. Create new alignments of strengths to make the institution's weaknesses irrelevant.

3. Refract human strengths such as compassion and wisdom out into society and the world.[11]

Cooperrider calls the VIA classification and survey a "classic" and says he uses it in all his executive work to "build a language for talking about strengths-based leadership." In the Appendix, you will find Illustration 2 to be a helpful tool for identifying and unleashing a team's strengths culture. Illustration 3 is an exercise created to help you identify and repeat the successes of a positive team experience.

Strengths Spotting

In addition to developing character strengths awareness, I coach people on how to recognize and appreciate character strengths in others. This not only gives them a renewed sense of themselves, but it also engages the most important people in their work and personal lives, in turn creating greater engagement and satisfaction for all. Train yourself to see these observable verbal and non-verbal cues that become apparent when a person is engaging his or her strengths:

Verbal Cues	Non-Verbal Cues
✓ Clearer Speech	✓ Increased Energy
✓ Faster Pace	✓ Improved Posture
✓ More Direct Communication	✓ Increased Eye Contact
✓ Larger Vocabulary	✓ Eyes Light Up
✓ Stronger Voice	✓ Increased Animation

Below are two notes I recently received from coaches who have built their strengths spotting capabilities:

It feels good to be recognized by others for who we are at our core; and when people make the effort to see these parts of us, we feel closer to them and more likely to return the favor by seeing what's best in them.

—Edwin Boom, Netherlands

I have begun to see strengths in people all the time. Last week while paying for my parking space, the parking lot attendant raced over to me because my work bag was hanging a little into the driveway. She had a sense of urgency, and you could tell she was very diligent in her role. My immediate thought was that she was high in prudence (caution) and that my car would always be very safe in her car parking lot. Perhaps if I were not a strength spotter, I'd see her urgency and actions differently!

—Jane Wundersitz, Australia

Appreciation Is Positive Feedback

Think of ways you can not only spot strengths in others, but also express appreciation of others' strengths at work. Make a list of systems that your team or organization can implement to better appreciate strengths. Recognizing strengths in fellow team members boosts group cohesion and morale. Because the language of strengths is somewhat new to many, it can be awkward at first to give others positive feedback in a genuine way. As you strive to help change your organization's culture (which, if yours is like most, has been focusing on what's wrong), consider the following four points:

Language: Words matter and so does how they are delivered. You don't want to come off as insincere when you are trying to encourage and offer words of affirmation. Try to describe the strengths in your own words. For example, when highlighting a colleague's perseverance, say, "I'm impressed with how you stuck with this problem until you found a solution."

Specificity: The more specific you can be with your praise, the more affirmed people feel. Generalities come across as lazy. When you are detailed, you signal that you've paid attention and appreciate the other person's efforts. To make your appreciative words meaningful, give feedback that is tied to specific behaviors. "You were so brave when you asserted your opinion in the meeting this morning."

Public vs. Private: For some people recognition in front of their peers or on a group email can heighten its meaning, while others prefer for such feedback to be offered privately. Care enough to be in tune with which delivery method will be most meaningful to the person you are addressing.

Frequency: People vary in how often they want positive feedback. For some, providing positive feedback only occasionally conveys more meaning, while others prefer frequent positive feedback—*i.e.* weekly or monthly.

So it's really a matter of communicating with one another and understanding what works for each person. Some organizations give their employees a questionnaire and ask employees to specify how they prefer to receive appreciation/recognition.

I am certainly not suggesting that everything in a work setting is always positive. I recognize that negative things happen at work and in life. People fall short. We get disappointed and frustrated with ourselves and with others. We shouldn't ignore problems as they occur.

But we do want to increase our awareness of the ratio of positives to negatives overall. Achieving this requires paying attention to what is going well. When people put their character strengths into action, engagement will result. When people are engaged, they will shine and in turn illuminate those around them. This ultimately results in what Dr. Mayerson calls an "illuminated workforce," operating at peak performance levels. A person can see more of his colleagues' strengths when he is illuminating the environment with his own strengths, and his positivity will be a guide—like a lighthouse—that will illuminate the way for others to activate their character strengths at work.

Coaching Tip

Look for ways that your strengths can contribute to your team's goals. It's a shift in perspective that will take you to new and more productive heights.

STRONG Questions©: Positive Team

- Where do my strengths align with my team/organization mission/values?
- What team functions do my strengths help me serve on my team?
- When do I find it most important to step up and/or make room for others?
- Which of my strengths have contributed to the "success factors" in a past positive team experience?
- How can I bring the learning from a past positive team experience to my current challenge/opportunity?
- How can I leave more of my signature on my work to make my contribution?
- How can I better notice/appreciate strengths in coworkers?

That which we persist in doing becomes easier for us to do; not that the nature of the thing itself is changed, but our power to do is INCREASED

Ralph Waldo Emerson

11 | FLOW WITH STRENGTHS

"Flow—the kind of knowledge or wisdom one needs for emancipating consciousness—is not cumulative. At least as much as intelligence, it requires the commitment of emotions and will. It is not enough to know how to do it; one must do it, consistently, in the same way as athletes and musicians who must keep practicing what they know in theory."

—Dr. Mihaly Csikszentmihalyi

Strengths engagement is based on the principle of positive progression, or the upward spiral. When we commit to expressing our character strengths optimally and consistently, we engage those strengths in a more authentic and natural expression. "Like Emerson's quote on the preceding page and Csikszentmihalyi's quote above, these positive practices literally increase our capacity to do. This upward spiral often produces what is commonly known as "flow."

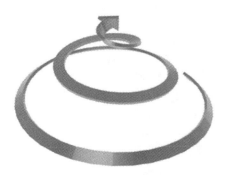

Exploring the richness of our strengths, empowering our goals with authentic strengths motivation, and engaging our strengths in our daily lives can produce a remarkable state of flow. What is flow? It is a movement characteristic of liquids. Water flows. When things flow, they are doing what they were made to do—think of a school of fish swimming. When flow is powerful and purposeful, you have optimal energy and full engagement. The resulting fulfillment you experience spills over into other areas of your life. You have learned to thrive.

What does a flow state look like? Think of Michael Phelps' arms churning through the water at the 2008 Olympics. He was "in the zone." In fact, watching any athlete achieve a peak experience is almost as exhilarating for the spectators as it is for the individual. It doesn't happen by accident. It requires practice, persistence, awareness, and optimal use of our character strengths. In order for springs to feed the streams that flow into the rivers that flow into the sea, conditions need to be cultivated. The stream needs an outlet or the water will become stagnant and dead. The river has cultivated a purposeful groove in the earth over time, and the channel must be open in order to empty into the realm of great possibilities.

In my coaching I work with people to cultivate the conditions to best express their character strengths so they can enjoy more flow in their work and personal lives. But make no mistake, my clients do the heavy lifting, which means they must carefully consider and identify how, when, with whom, and to what degree they choose to employ and develop their strengths. This responsibility builds their commitment. When they make this a consistent practice, it eventually becomes second nature; then, their strengths take on an intelligence of their own that enables them to flow.

Flowing with Strengths

When you are in flow, you have more energy and awareness. The landscape (inner and outer) looks sharper; everything is more focused. You find yourself completely immersed in what you are doing—you are savoring every moment, not wanting it to end. Think of a time you have experienced a "flow state." Perhaps it was while you were working on a project where you felt purposeful and made a significant contribution, or engaging in your favorite sport, or spending meaningful, quality time with loved ones.

I had an interesting discussion with Mihaly Csikszentmihalyi at an evening reception during the First World Congress on Positive Psychology. In his book, *Flow: The Psychology of Optimal Experience*, he identifies these criteria for being in a flow state: completely involved, a sense of ecstasy, great inner clarity, a belief that the job is doable, serenity, a sense of timelessness, and a feeling that the activity that produces the flow has intrinsic worth. Mihaly affirmed to me that the sense of meaning, purpose, and authenticity produced by our strengths enables flow. Research has shown that character strengths may occupy the most central role in the field of positive psychology, and that flow and other positive experiences are enabled by good character.[2]

We all know what it feels like when something "clicks" and we suddenly are able to see, understand, or act on something that previously had baffled us. Our senses are engaged. We feel elated. Ideas spark and explode like fireworks. For example, listening to my inner coach instead of my inner critic, I chose to enroll in the year-long advanced Columbia University Coaching Certification Program. A few years later, I found myself even more passionate about "being a contribution" to others and have felt completely energized while writing this book.

Being in flow with our strengths also creates a sense of happiness and well-being.[3] Famed positive psychologist Ed Diener, who is mentioned earlier in the book, commented to me once about what made him happy: "Analyzing data always makes me happy. Seriously. Possibly I am a weird person. But when I examine data, I almost always feel that I am discovering something new. And it is a quiet activity that is calm, and I can just think and examine what is going on in the world via the data."

Diener has found many productive methods of using his strengths. He has learned to put his authentic gifts to the best use, and that makes him happier than looking outside himself for fulfillment, i.e., over-indulging in some meaningless pleasure or pushing into overdrive to prove himself to others, or checking out altogether.

The biggest insight he told me he had in researching happiness was that "happiness is not just a place, but also a process. I once thought that when I had my 'ducks in a row,' the right wife, kids, house, and job, that I would be happy from then on. And of course those things all helped a lot. But I learned that happiness is an ongoing process of fresh challenges, and that even when everything is in place, it takes the right attitudes and activities to continue to be happy."[4]

The Mechanics of Flow

Essential to producing a flow state is learning how to relax enough to let it happen. However, true relaxation is rarely achieved passively. Studies show that stimulating the vagus nerve through deep breathing exercises (such as in mindfulness practices) can improve memory, focus, and produce a general sense of well-being, not to mention provide quick relief from stress and anxiety.

The "relaxation response" happens when the vagus nerve—which flows from your brain through your neck and chest and diaphragm—turns on the parasympathetic nervous system during inhalation, cortisol levels drop and the brain relaxes. Relaxed, but alert, trained monks can maintain intricate mental images with no loss of details for hours.

In his bestseller, *The Relaxation Response*, Harvard Medical School cardiologist Herbert Benson describes how even simplified forms of meditation produce physiological benefits such as reduced heart, metabolic, and breathing rates. More recent studies have linked meditation and its physiological benefits with more acute mental focus, freedom from negative judgments, and increased compassion.[5]

Research by Richard Davidson—the neuroscientist at the University of Wisconsin-Madison, who used functional magnetic-resonance imaging (MRI) on monks—demonstrated the dynamics of this brain activity: positive states of mind are marked by high activity in the left frontal area, while activity in the right frontal area coincides with negative states. The monks could induce a state of compassion in themselves, illustrated by a much greater shift toward left frontal brain activity, which subjects untrained in meditation could not.[6]

> Not only can we control our consciousness, but we can reshape our brains.

Why is this so exciting? It is proof that humans can control their consciousness. Not only can we control our consciousness, but we can reshape our brains. This is the beauty of the "neuroplasticity" discussed in chapter three. We can choose to develop beneficial centers in our brain by consciously stimulating neural activity in those areas and quieting blood flow to areas that produce anxiety, stress, depression, etc. We can also create habits of positive chemical release by looking at all aspects of our lives through the lens of our character strengths—work, relationships and health can be transformed in this way. Living authentically, by giving expression to our character strengths, is a powerful way to induce relaxation and enable flow.

Flow and Contribution

When we ask, "What are the needs I see around me?" what begins to emerge is the contribution we can make, the service we can render. When this service is grounded in and powered by the most authentic part of ourselves, our character strengths, we are in the position to make a valuable contribution.[7] The best solutions or contributions in society, in business, and in personal life have emerged when people apply their strengths to serving a need. For me, my passion is coaching people to live vibrant, flourishing, whole lives. I love to help people use their character strengths to achieve their highest level of performance and satisfaction in all areas of their lives.

It seems easy on the surface, but oftentimes we get so busy in day-to-day life that we don't even know what we are passionate about any more. We have probably disconnected from those strengths that enliven us. How do we bring passion and flow back into day-to-day life? I like to ask my clients, "What have you always loved doing? What feels like play to you, so that when you engage in that activity, time seems to fly by, and you feel happier and uplifted? If you were financially independent, what would you choose to do with your time? Think blue sky here. What is happening around you that you care about deeply—in your workplace, in your family, in your relationships, in your community?" Answering questions like these is a step toward reconnecting with your authentic strengths and enabling flow.

Is it possible that a great opportunity can line up with your character strengths and you are excited about it, but your inner coach says no? Absolutely. I have a coaching client, a very talented woman with two young children. She decided to forego a lucrative and enticing career that involved a lot of travel. She chose to work part-time from home instead, because she wanted to enjoy and contribute fully to her children's upbringing. This doesn't mean she will never pursue those particular career strengths and passions; it just means that, for now, she chooses to focus her strengths within the walls of her own home. This season in her life is too important to miss.

Flowing Toward Insight

When in a flow state, writers write unforgettable stories, musicians create memorable music, artists paint masterpieces, and scientists study everything around them. Great moments in insight history include Archimedes shouting "Eureka!" when he saw his bathwater rise and Isaac Newton understanding gravity as an apple fell from a tree.

What happens inside the brain to produce insight? Jonah Lehrer wrote about "The Eureka Hunt" in a New Yorker article pointing to cognitive neuroscientist Mark Jung-Beeman of Northwestern University who studied the "insight" phenomenon for many years—mapping the brain's circuitry.[8] Combining EEG with MRI, he found that subjects in a study who solved puzzles using insight activated a specific subset of cortical areas. First the brain tries to block out distractions, focusing on the problem to be solved. Then the brain looks for answers. An insight often comes just before the brain is ready to give up, when it finally lets go of the problem and relaxes, spiking the gamma rhythm, which is the highest electrical frequency generated by the brain.

Many conclude that the best way to produce an insight might be to let the mind wander or take a warm shower (because the relaxation phase is crucial). However, it seems that this works only if you have focused on the solution until you are at an impasse and, ready to give up, you finally relax enough to receive the answer. Insights are one of the secrets of the prefrontal cortex about which we hope to learn more.

Another ideal moment for insights, according to scientists, is the early morning right after we wake up. The drowsy brain is relaxed, unwound, and disorganized, open to all sorts of unconventional ideas. The right hemisphere is also unusually active. Try not to let the morning rush squash your creative insights. Build in some time in your morning to wake up slowly and simply lie still and think creatively before you have to get out of bed.

> Trying to force an insight by over-focusing on a problem can actually prevent the insight.

Trying to force an insight by over-focusing on a problem can actually prevent the insight. Rather, a holistic, positive, strengths-oriented approach appears to produce better results. Research has recently demonstrated that making people focus on the details of a visual scene, as opposed to the big picture, can significantly disrupt the insight process. If you work in a stressful overachieve, overdrive environment and don't build in relaxation breaks to step back and clear your head, you may find your creativity slumping. Many of the most forward-thinking companies, like Google, understand this and provide relaxation activities at work to enable creativity and insight. The data is in—people who are in a good mood are much better at solving puzzles and developing creative solutions.

Strengths Flow: Real Wealth

In his book, *Happiness—Unlocking the Mysteries of Psychological Wealth*, Ed Diener talks about our outlook on work and how it can affect our happiness, our performance, and ultimately our well-being. Based on his extensive research, he describes three orientations to work: we can see work as a job, a career, or a calling. When we see work as a job, we view leisure as more important, we are motivated by money, we would not recommend the work unless required, we do what we are told, and we look forward to the end of each shift. When we see work as a career, we might enjoy the work, we are motivated by advancement, we may recommend the work, we think a lot about vacations, we take initiative to impress supervisors, and we work hard for possible advancement. In contrast, when we see work as a calling, we enjoy our work, we are motivated by and express our character strengths at work, we see our strengths as a way to make a meaningful contribution, we recommend the work, we think about work even off the clock, we work hard because we find the job rewarding, and doing our job well is intrinsically motivating.[10]

So why don't we raise the quality of our lives by finding ways to utilize our strengths more at work and transform it into a calling? We can "practice" putting ourselves in a state conducive to flow—the positive, clear thinking that can feed creativity.

Positive Practices Enable Flow

Great athletes, peak performers, and true leaders rely on regular practice to achieve optimum experiences. The same can be true of anyone whose life is grounded in regularly expressing and appreciating character strengths. I call these "positive practices." Every time we participate in a positive practice, we are expressing our commitment to empower and engage our strengths and to appreciate strengths in others. Families who sit down to dinner together regularly are saying without words that they believe in the need for families to have shared time together. Organizations that provide regular outlets for expression and appreciation of strengths are communicating that they invest in their people and want to develop their potential.

Far from precluding spontaneity, positive practices provide a level of comfort, continuity, and security that frees us to improvise and to take risks. Think of a great athlete producing a seemingly impossible shot under fierce pressure, a highly trained surgeon making a critical counterintuitive decision at a life or death moment during a delicate operation, or an executive breaking an impasse in a difficult, formal negotiation by suddenly coming up with a novel structure for a deal. Positive practices provide a stable framework for utilizing our strengths and enabling creative breakthroughs to occur. They can also open up time for renewal of our strengths, when relationships can be deepened, and reflection and growth become possible.

In other words, we can "train" for greatness. Much as it is possible to strengthen a muscle by subjecting it to stress and recovery, we can develop our ability to utilize and leverage our strengths. By building positive practices that become automatic—and subsequently relatively effortless—we ensure a strong showing in any pursuit to which we turn our efforts.

A positive practice I engage in regularly with my clients is the 3 R's©. At the end of each week, clients *reflect* on progress made, *reveal* any valuable insights gained that they can leverage going forward, and *recalibrate* future actions accordingly. This process fuels the upward spiral, which is why the upward spiral is placed at the center of the 3 R's© Model below. The 3 R's© and the upward spiral work together to engage our strengths.

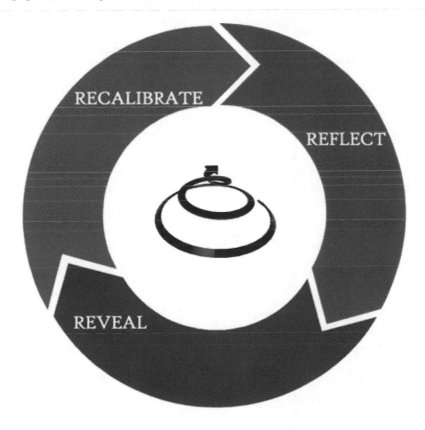

Authentic Strengths 3 R's Model. © Authentic Strengths Advantage, 2014.)

STRONG Questions©: Reflect, Reveal, Recalibrate

REFLECT on Progress

✓ What progress have I made on action commitments?

✓ How do I feel about my progress?

✓ If this is a growth milestone, how will I celebrate?

REVEAL Insights

✓ What is the impact of my actions? What did I learn?

✓ How do I feel about my goal(s) now?

✓ What got in the way of me realizing my action commitment?

RECALIBRATE When Necessary

✓ What actions make sense to continue?

✓ What actions should be stopped or changed?

✓ What new actions might I consider starting?

✓ What strengths can I use or build to help achieve my goal(s)?

Living and Working in Flow

Sir Richard Branson has never been afraid to challenge conventions. You wouldn't know it from seeing his list of achievements and his face plastered on ads, but he is by nature rather shy. He is dyslexic, which resulted in poor academic performance as a child. But he discovered he was good at making connections with people despite his shyness.

His companies have had their ups and downs, but in 1992 he sold the Virgin label to EMI for $1 billion to fund Virgin Airlines. Today, the Virgin group operates in fifty countries and has made over $24 billion.[11]

How does Branson keep it all going? He's in the flow. He takes time with his family to recharge. He practices the skills he needs for keeping his brain and body in a dynamic balance. Everything we do is based on an easily depleted reservoir of energy. Rituals extend and renew that energy. Active rest and relaxation are as important a ritual as any of the others.

Branson does not stand on ceremony when he is ready to be flooded with ideas. If he's in a meeting, he may go lie down on a couch and continue brainstorming with his guest. If he hears a great idea and doesn't have a notebook handy, he'll jot it down on the back of his hand. What matters to him is the free flow of ideas, and he does whatever it takes to keep the tap flowing.

Even if you're not the head of a company, there are ways to foster and facilitate your creativity similar to what Branson does. Maybe you can't lie down on a couch during a meeting, but perhaps you can take a break and briskly walk up and down a hallway or sprint around the building or go to the restroom and run cold water over your wrists—whatever changes the dynamic of feeling "stuck." Maybe you can't take a full month off every year to renew, but do take advantage of earned vacation and sick time when you need it, instead of hoarding it or passing over it thinking you can't afford to take it. The truth is you can't afford not to. Change your setting and be stimulated by new surroundings that might lead to creative new thoughts. By repeating any of the positive practices found in this chapter, or others that we discover work for us, we can strengthen our ability to enter into and remain in a flow state of creativity.

Strengths Flow

In the ASA Strengths Flow© model below I have distilled the key elements of flow, and connected them with the emerging research on character strengths into a simplified model that my clients find easy to understand and to use.

Authenticity
- Strengths Expression - using character strengths authentically is energizing.
- Strengths Optimization - be mindful of expressing strengths in the "optimal" zone - avoiding extremes of overuse and underuse.

Positive Practices
- Developed Skill - invest time and effort to develop a skill over time so that it becomes second nature.
- Consistent Gains - positive practices continually increase effectiveness.

Connection
- Meaning/Purpose - a strong sense of purpose, serenity and connection to something larger than self.
- Intrinsic Motivation - engaging in the activity for the pure joy of it—compensation is not the focus.
- Passion - the activity produces a sense of ecstasy, happiness and timelessness; hours can feel like minutes.

Challenge
- Growth - The activity is challenging, but is "doable" and not anxiety producing.
- Energized Focus - relaxed yet engaged—enabling spontaneity and creativity.

Exercise Strengths Flow©

Below is an exercise I created for my clients who are stressed, disconnected or experiencing blocks to flow. I encourage them to practice deep breathing techniques as they use this exercise to relax, increase their focus and enable flow.

Breathing in, "I feel calm."
Breathing out, "I relax."
Breathing in, "I appreciate my strengths."
Breathing out, "I am centered."
Breathing in, "I see the big picture."
Breathing out, "I am at ease."
Breathing in, "my mind is clear."
Breathing out, "I am energized."

Coaching Tip

Harness your strengths to enable flow. Ask the coaching questions below to help you and others achieve more flow personally and professionally.

STRONG Questions©: Flow

- What activities am I passionate about? Which ones energize me?
- What activities do I dread/avoid? Which ones deplete me?
- What strengths do I typically express in my energizing activities?
- How do my strengths benefit me/others? Have others noticed?
- How can my strengths help me flow through challenges, personally/professionally?
- What changes have resulted since I began to use my strengths in new ways?
- What one positive practice could I begin today to produce better results in my life?

Fame is a vapor, popularity an accident, riches take wings, and only

CHARACTER

endures.

Horace Greeley

12 | RIDE THE WAVE TO UNCOMMON PERFORMANCE

"A good character carries with it the highest power of causing a thing to be believed."

—*Aristotle*

"Character is like a tree and reputation like its shadow. The shadow is what we think of it; the tree is the real thing."

—*Abraham Lincoln*

"The development and expression of character strengths are now known to be among the most important strategies we have for achieving our positive life potential."

—*Dr. Neal H. Mayerson*

Sam Bracken, the colleague I mentioned earlier, has the build of an NFL player. He is currently the global director of marketing at a large company. Years ago, he was on track at Georgia Tech University to play in the NFL when injuries sidelined his football career. Was this twist of fate the ultimate irony for Sam, who had managed to survive a childhood of unspeakable abuse? Sam had lived a fringe existence in the jumble of trailer parks and rundown apartments in Las Vegas.

Lit on fire at the age of five by a sadistic older boy who soon became his stepbrother, homeless at times, stuck in special education classes because no one ever checked to find out he needed glasses to read, Sam was drinking and using drugs by the age of nine.

His survival had always depended on his ability to focus on the positive while living in the seamy, bleak underbelly of society. Once he made up his mind to change and was old enough to act on his desire for a different life, his academics improved and he won a football scholarship to Georgia Tech. After an outstanding freshman year, he suffered shoulder injuries that might have ended his career. He healed through a rigorous commitment to self-improvement and eventually re-earned his starting position on one of Georgia Tech's most successful football teams. Sam forged his own path, but he had the help of a very special coach at Georgia Tech who guided him to develop his strengths of character as a whole person, not just an athlete. Now Sam uses his strengths as he teaches others about excellence, leadership, and change.

Sam is an example of how an at-risk, terribly abused child became a leader and coach himself, changing his fate one thought at a time with the help of a dedicated, thoughtful, and kind coach who recognized and appreciated the best in Sam—his strengths.

Build Strengths to Ride the Wave

Coaching is a little like teaching surfing. First of all, you and the person you coach must train to be in good shape because it's a long paddle to the good waves. Your mind and body need to be sharp as well as alert to both optimum and dangerous conditions. Second, you've got to have great balance to stay on top of the swells. Third, you need to trust that when you get up on your feet to ride the wave, you can do it.

Surfing instructors don't just push people into the waves and yell, "Stand up!" Nor do smart coaches fling people into challenging life and work situations and yell from the sidelines without adequate preparation and practice.

When a person receives great one-on-one coaching, performance often improves dramatically. For example, training alone increases productivity by more than twenty-two percent; but when followed by one-on-one coaching, that figure soars to eighty-eight percent, according to *Public Personnel Management, The Business Case for Coaching.*[2]

Coaching to uncommon performance revolves around several principles: acknowledging the person being coached is creative, resourceful and whole; focusing on authentic character strengths instead of weaknesses and failings; and accountability to agreed-upon standards.

Great coaching is not about giving advice, sharing experiences, supervising or managing. It is not about "fixing" people, but about seeing potential and communicating that effectively. It's about bringing out the best in someone and spotlighting character strengths that have been underexposed.

Remember, the way a butterfly gets strong is by struggling to break out of its chrysalis. If you interfere with the process you end up crippling the butterfly, which needs the resistance to strengthen its wings. Savvy coaches don't jump in and try to do the hard work for the person being coached. Instead, they acknowledge that growth can be painful and they encourage stretching, strengthening, and reaching toward optimum experiences and balanced living. A great way to do this is to intentionally build upon the strengths we need for the challenge at hand. I have included some strengths-building strategies for you on the following page.

> It's about bringing out the best in someone and spotlighting natural strengths that have been underexposed.

Build Your Strengths

Below are some suggested activities to jump-start you in building any of the twenty-four character strengths you choose to increase. Don't feel constrained to this list. You can design whatever activity you think will work for you, as long as it allows you to build a strength of your choosing.

Curiosity
o Ask a question.
o Discover new places or try a new food.
o Explore your local library or an e-learning site.

Love of Learning
o Read a new newspaper or magazine.
o Explore new learning sites you never otherwise would have discovered.
o Every day, read a chapter of a book on a new topic.

Judgment (Critical Thinking)
o Play devil's advocate and discuss an issue from the opposing side to your personal views.
o Go to lunch with someone who is different from you in some way.
o Every day, pick something you believe strongly, and think about other possible perspectives.

Creativity
o Keep a journal, write a poem or a literary piece, or decorate a living space.
o Pick one object in your room and devise another use for it rather than its intended use.
o Find a new word every day and use it creatively.

Social Intelligence
o Meet one new person each day by initiating a conversation.
o Whenever talking to someone, be aware of your behavior and how you are being perceived.
o When talking to people, try to understand their perspective on what you are discussing.

Perspective (Wisdom)
o Find one new quote each day online.
o Think of the wisest person you know. Try to live each day as that person would live.
o Look up prominent people in history and learn their views on important issues of their day.

Bravery
o Speak up (with tact) for an unpopular idea (if you believe in it).
o Invite someone new on an outing.
o Introduce yourself to a stranger at work, class or a party.

Perseverance
o Notice why you are tempted to stop a task. Resolve to focus on the task.
o Plan ahead. Use a calendar for tasks.
o Set a challenging goal and stick to it.

Honesty (Authenticity)
- Notice each time you exaggerate in conversation and correct the exaggeration.
- Refrain from telling small, white lies and give only sincere compliments and praise.
- Make a daily list of every time you tell even a small lie. Make your list shorter every day.

Zest (Enthusiasm and Energy)
- Volunteer for a new cause or become more involved in an organization you are already a part of.
- Get adequate rest and good nutrition to increase your energy.
- Do something physically vigorous.

Kindness (Generosity)
- Leave a large tip for a small check.
- Do a small, random act of anonymous kindness every day, like sending an e-card.
- Be a listening ear to a friend.

Capacity to Love and Be Loved
- Tell someone you love that you love them or give them a hug.
- Send a loved one a card/e-card to say you were thinking about him/her.
- Write a nice note to someone you care about.

Teamwork (Citizenship)
- Pick up litter that you see on the ground.
- Contribute your best attitude, work, information and ideas to a project.
- Organize a team lunch.

Fairness
- Allow someone to speak her piece while keeping an open mind by not passing judgment.
- Stay impartial in an argument between friends despite your beliefs (be the mediator).
- Notice when you treat someone based on a stereotype/pre-conception; resolve not to do it again.

Leadership
- Organize something special for your friends one evening.
- Form a community group to tackle issues in your area or start a book club.
- Encourage a group to do its best work.

Self-Control and Self-Regulation
- Work out regularly or stick to better eating habits for a week.
- When something upsets you, refute negative thoughts and use calming activities.
- Make a resolution to not gossip. When you feel the urge, remember your resolution and stop.
- Make an agenda for the following day. Stick to that agenda.
- Think twice before speaking and consider the effect of your words on others.
- Think about the motto "Better safe than sorry" at least three times a day.
- Before making important decisions, consider the impact in one day or one year later.

Modesty
- Don't talk about yourself at all for a full day.
- Dress and act modestly, so as not to attract attention to yourself.
- Find something someone you know is better at than you. Compliment them for it.

Prudence (Discretion)
- o Think twice before speaking and consider the effect of your words on others.
- o Think about the motto "Better safe than sorry" at least three times a day.
- o Before making important decisions, consider the impact in one day or one year later.

Forgiveness
- o Think of someone that you find hard to forgive. Try to see the situation from that person's perspective. Consider if you had made the same mistake, would you have wanted to be forgiven?
- o Make contact with someone who upset you in the past. Let him know that you forgive him, or just be kind to that person in your conversation.
- o When someone does something that upsets you, try to fathom his or her intentions in the actions. Assume the best and do not assign bad motives.

Appreciation of Beauty/Excellence
- o Go to a museum and admire artwork that touches you because of its beauty and aesthetics.
- o Take a walk and appreciate something beautiful in nature.
- o Attend a concert or listen to a new song to enjoy music for its creative value.

Gratitude
- o Keep a journal, and each night, make a list of three things that you are thankful for in life.
- o Every day, thank someone for something that you might otherwise take for granted.
- o Keep a record of the number of times you use the words "thank you" in a day. Over the course of the first week, try to double the number of times that you say those words.

Hope (Optimism)
- o Keep a daily journal and record decisions that will positively impact your life.
- o When you are in a bad situation, try to see the optimistic side of it, even if only for the learning.
- o Notice your negative thoughts. Counter them with positive thoughts.

Spirituality (Sense of Purpose)
- o Make a list of things you can do to improve the world or your community.
- o Read a spiritual book, attend a religious service or engage in meditation/prayer.
- o Read from a book of affirmations or optimistic quotes each day.

Humor (Playfulness)
- o Every day, try to make someone smile or laugh.
- o Learn a joke or magic trick and share it with your friends.
- o Watch a funny movie or TV show or read the comics.

Adapted from VIA Classification of Character Strengths, Strengths Building

Below is an inspiring letter received from A. Lyle, an individual who applied the strengths-building ideas in this chapter:

> Strengths coaching was a real eye-opener for me. It revealed several underutilized strengths that were preventing me from fully implementing some of my signature strengths. Of my top strengths, two of them are curiosity and love of learning, while one of my lowest-ranked strengths is perseverance. All of a sudden I realized why I am constantly starting fascinating intellectual writing projects and never completing them. I abandon the old idea or project because I'm so excited about learning about a new one; and with little perseverance, it's a perfect storm for never finishing anything I start. In fact, I had become so discouraged over the years that I was to the point of not even starting anything—assuming I wouldn't finish.
>
> Another top strength is kindness, driving me to be genuinely interested in helping people and wishing I could make an impact on their lives. But with social intelligence ranked almost dead last in my strengths ranking, I often don't connect with people the way I would love to.
>
> I always assumed these were character flaws that were an unchangeable part of my personality. Then I read *Authentic Strengths* and realized that my strengths ranking wasn't set in stone. I have all twenty-four strengths, and I can build upon my lesser strengths! I may have been neglecting some of them, but they're all at my disposal. This idea really motivated me, and I decided to test it one morning. Instead of my usual minimal "medium starch" and no eye-contact interaction with the attendant at my neighborhood cleaners, I consciously decided to test using two of my signature strengths, curiosity and kindness, to raise my social intelligence. Well, after twenty years "Carla" and I now greet each other by name, and I will be interested next time I drop off cleaning to hear about her Disneyland trip with her daughter. And my errands will go from automated to energizing because of the genuine human connection.

Buoyed by this simple success, I'm also working on that never-finishing-anything weakness. Perseverance has taken on tremendous importance for me—I now truly care about finishing what I start. I even keep a list by my desk of everything I finish. Projects big and small that never made it past the good idea stage are now making the list of accomplishments—everything from planting a rose in honor of my mother to web-publishing past speeches—and each thing I complete returns the energy of accomplishment rather than the dejection of unfinished failure.

Raking the Sand

When the tide goes out, it leaves things behind on the shore. Some are worth keeping, and others we leave behind to be carried back out to sea by the next wave. A good time to take inventory of our character strengths and reflect on how to better use them in the future is after we've "ridden the big one" up onto shore and the ebbing tide has left some things in plain view on the sand. What authentic strengths do we see that propelled us to new heights? These are the ones we should pick up off the sand and polish.

I coached a man who had some major breakthroughs in his work life as he examined the shore. He came to recognize that he was a perfectionist who micromanaged everyone's work. This kept him so busy that he was out of the flow of doing the creative thinking he was best at. He learned to set clear end-result expectations and then get out of the way of his staff. He learned he could not hold people accountable to results when he nitpicked their methods. The time and space this opened up for him was enormous. He unleashed his creative energy and went on to successfully develop and launch two new "big ideas" for his business. He doubled his business that year, something he would never have done had he been looking over everyone's shoulder, worrying and obsessing that they weren't doing it "his" way.

You can't sift through the evidence of your life, however, unless you get out and walk the shore regularly. Make an appointment with yourself to reflect on your goals. In order to do that you have to know what you have in inventory—in your pockets, in your head, at your fingertips, and lying in the sand at your feet waiting to be picked up.

Paddling Out: Strengths Coaching

My friend Sam did not make all the changes in his life on his own. His wise football coach saw him as a young man with great potential, but not only as an athlete. The coach did not do the work for Sam. He pointed out to Sam some things he could do for himself, starting with helping him map where he was at the moment and where he wanted to be—then coming up with a plan to get there.

The wave you have to ride might come from outside of you, but the ability to ride it comes from inside of you—from your authentic character strengths. There is no balance without strength and focus, and if your stamina is not up to par, it's going to be a difficult ride.

That's where a coach comes in.

Everyone from Michael Jordan to Cardinal Richelieu has used a coach to reach greatness. In a study published in the *Harvard Business Review,* "What Coaches Can Do for You,"[4] the top reason executive coaches are hired is to develop high potential or to facilitate transition (forty-eight percent) followed by acting as a sounding board (twenty-six percent). Although they are rarely hired to deal with personal issues, seventy-six percent of coaches say that they assist executives with personal issues. The reason for that is because personal issues often surface as the factors that are holding back professional development.

> **Strengths coaching works because it not only helps you create positive practices to be your best, but because your coach paddles out alongside you to the wave you have chosen.**

Strengths coaching works because it not only helps you create positive practices in order to be your best, but because your coach paddles out alongside you to the wave you have carefully chosen. Once there, you stand or fall on your own, with the understanding that you will be able to get up and try again. The coach is not a safety net, but carries a life preserver at the ready in case you need it. The life preserver is the coach's knowledge of your strengths, everything she or he has observed. If you falter, the coach will remind you of who you are and what you can do—redirecting troubling thoughts into a positive framework. The only agenda is to be in the flow. Ride the wave.

Balancing on the Board: Trust

Most everyone can relate to times they did something really hard and unavoidable. Staying on top of that wave is the answer—accepting the moment for what it is, and trusting that you will emerge better for it.

How do you do that? By using your mind to focus on the goal, which you have visualized and decided on beforehand. By putting your trust in what you have practiced repeatedly and anchoring those positive practices in your character strengths.[4] And by focusing on that one image: staying on top of the wave. Try this simple "one week challenge" below to build your ability to ride the wave.

Exercise: One-Week Challenge—Choose & Use[5]

Here is a popular exercise from positive psychology to use your strengths in new ways for just one week and get measurable, positive results. Studies show this one exercise can significantly increase your sense of happiness and well-being, while decreasing anxiety and depression. The measurable mood boost people get from this exercise tends to last about six months![6]

1. List your top (signature) strengths.

2. Pick one or two.

3. Look for ways to use the strength(s) daily for a week.

Trust in yourself, like balance, can be built from the ground up when you align your character strengths with your goals and act on them. Gandhi said, "To believe in something, and not to live it, is dishonest." When your character is your message, you both inspire and attract trust. Everything is just too slippery without it.

Riding the Wave

*"Promise me you will not spend so much time treading water
and trying to keep your head above the waves that you forget
how much you have always loved to swim."*

—*Tyler Knott Gregson*

Riding the wave frightens a lot of people. Seeing something coming toward you that has the power to take you down is equivalent to facing a crisis point—whether it's a wall of water, losing your job if you don't improve your performance, feeling you have lost respect and authority in your family, or undergoing chemotherapy. But what if you could welcome that wave and learn to ride it to new heights? Beyond the fear lies the ecstasy of tackling the Big Kahuna.

Big waves and other challenges must be sized up and respected for their power. You want to be prepared for the challenge in body, mind, heart, and spirit. And sometimes you have to back away. Conditions may not allow a ride.

But if you have explored, empowered, and engaged your character strengths, you have learned to focus on what's strong instead of what's wrong. You can now see obstacles as opportunities—you can harness the winds of adversity to propel yourself toward your desired destination. With each new challenge, you can learn and grow and progress.

A friend of mine had an unexpected opportunity to go to St. Martin for a weekend with her twenty-one-year-old son. Her son was a single father with joint custody, and my friend was helping him raise his daughter in their family home.

Mother and son went out on a group wave runner tour one morning, both on the same Jet Ski. The aqua Caribbean Sea was transparent and calm. As they rounded a cliff the water got choppy, then rough. Waves started slapping the mother in the face. Riding on the back of the Jet Ski with her arms wrapped tightly around her son's waist, she saw the waves get higher and higher. They'd coast up to the crest and then fall, slamming into the water and climbing the next wave almost before she could catch her breath. As her son wrestled the Jet Ski from crest to crest, he kept turning his head and yelling at her.

Due to the rough waters, they had traveled far from shore and gotten separated from the group, but finally the shoreline came into view around a bend. The waves subsided, and the mother, drained but grateful for her son's expert steering, finally heard what her son had been yelling each time he'd turned around: "Mom, isn't this beautiful!" Hearing his words made her realize something important.

During her son's childhood, the waves in her own path had been high—and it was her son who had been hanging on for dear life behind her as they rode from wave to wave. She had done her best to encourage him through those hard times to engage his own strengths in order to see the beauty of the ride.

Looking back, she realized that although the Jet Ski experience had been the ride of her life, she had been in good hands. Her son was up to the task. He had the ability to ride those rough waves just the way he had displayed his ability to raise his daughter in less-than-perfect circumstances. He had become an extraordinary father, a good student, and a responsible worker. Just as she was proud of the way he had handled the Jet Ski so capably in treacherous waters, she was also proud of the way he was using his authentic strengths to ride the waves in his life to shore.

13 | APPENDIX

VIA Character Strengths in Rank Order

This graph depicts the character strengths ordered by average raw score: 5 - "Very much like me," 4 - "Like me," 3 - "Not like or unlike me," 2 - "Unlike me," and 1 - "Very much unlike me." This is a sample graph for a fictitious person provided here to give you a visual of what your graph may look like.

Illustration 1

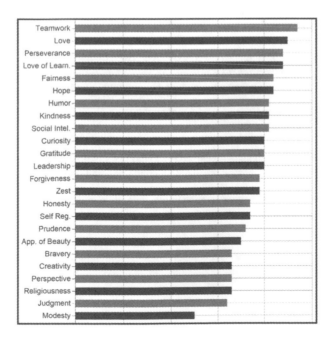

VIA Character Strengths in Rank Order (© VIA Institute on Character, 2014.) All rights reserved. Used with permission.)

Illustration 2

Strengths Culture

Below are tips to identify and unleash a team's strengths culture:

- Which strengths best define the team's culture?

- How does the team's culture compare with the organization's overall culture? Are the two cultures compatible or at odds with one another?

- How does the team's culture affect the team's functioning?

- How does the team's culture affect each person's performance and feelings about the group? Do they feel more encouraged and included or discouraged and excluded?

- While working on a values and/or mission statement, ensure that all team members have at least one of their top strengths reflected in the statement that is created.

Illustration 3

Exercise: Positive Team

Think of a time where you had a positive team experience—when everyone on the team was engaged and accomplished a goal that was meaningful.

- What were the success factors?

- Describe the work environment.

- What were the interpersonal dynamics: strengths, roles, personalities?

- Was there clarity of purpose? Describe.

- Were strengths appreciated and leveraged?

ACKNOWLEDGEMENTS

It is with heartfelt thanks that I acknowledge the many people who have helped make this book possible. I am deeply grateful to my husband Rob and my sons Kaden and Sage for their unconditional love and encouragement. Words cannot express how much I adore them, and my heart is full with the joy they bring into my life daily.

To my parents, Tiberio and Isabel Silveira, for the courage, perseverance and hope they exercised when faced with uncommon challenges. They left behind their country of birth in order to provide greater opportunities and a better life for our family. I love them deeply and will always be humbled by and grateful for their selfless contribution.

To my siblings whom I love tremendously and with whom I have so much fun—Phyllis Camboia, Joe Silveira, Isabel Pierce and Laurette Eslinger—you have always encouraged and supported me. We have comforted each other through life's difficulties, and I am grateful for the beautiful bond we share.

To Dr. Neal H. Mayerson and Donna Mayerson whose service to the cause of strengths education is helping to build a better world. I greatly appreciate your dedication to the mission of the VIA Institute on Character. And to Dr. Ryan Niemiec, Breta Cooper and Kelly Alluise at the VIA Institute on Character who work diligently to spread the empowering message of character strengths to the world.

To Dr. Martin E.P. Seligman, whose groundbreaking work in the field of positive psychology and hopeful message to the world inspired me to write this book.

To my friends and colleagues, David Covey and Stephan Mardyks, whose significant work at SMCOV helping content providers to share their empowering messages is increasing engagement and improving the way people do business around the world.

To the Columbia University Coaching Certification Program and my friend and colleague, Dr. Terry Maltbia, who continues to inspire me toward coaching excellence. Your brilliant thought leadership, guidance, and contributions to the field of executive coaching have been invaluable.

To Tiffany Yoast, my incredibly gifted, intelligent friend and colleague who helped me as a sounding board during the countless hours I discussed new tools and theories with her. Her beautiful work on the book design is greatly appreciated, but more than that, her collaboration and insights were invaluable.

To Echo Garrett, my friend and colleague, whose artistic and beautiful writing style helped massage book content into thought-provoking, enjoyable reading.

To Liz Patterson, my friend and colleague with whom I discuss positive psychology coaching principles and application. Her coaching insights and wise counsel are greatly appreciated.

I am humbled by the many friends and colleagues who supported me through their reading of the manuscript and by providing their helpful feedback and design suggestions, namely Tiffany Yoast, David Covey, Stephan Mardyks, Dr. Neal Mayerson, Dr. Ryan Neimiec, Ally Lyle, Ann Larsen, Isabel Silveira, Jeanne Elliott, Kristen Walton, Liz Patterson, Jane Wundersitz, Judy Bell, Trish Barrus, J. Goodman Farr, Lisa Lambert, Lisa Cook, Morgan Pitcher, Dr. Felicia English and Heather Moon.

NOTES AND REFERENCES

Introduction

1. Towers Watson. "Global Workforce Study." Boston: Towers Watson, 2012.

2. Sorenson, Susan. "How Employees' Strengths Make Your Company Stronger" Gallup Business Journal, last modified Feb 20, 2014, http://www.gallup.com/businessjournal/167462/ employees-strengths-company-stronger.aspx.

3. International Coach Federation. 2014 ICF Global Consumer Awareness Study. Harrodsburg, KY: ICF, 2014.

Part 1
Chapter 1: Silence the Critic, Discover the Coach

1. Allmendinger, Jutta, J. Richard Hackman, and Erin V. Lehman. "Life and Work in Symphony Orchestras," *The Music Quarterly* 80, no. 2 (1996): 194-219.

2. Frankl, Viktor. "Man's Search for Meaning." Boston: Beacon Press, 2006.

3. Grant, A. M. (2003). The impact of coaching on goal attainment, meta-cognition, and mental health. *Social Behavior and Personality, 31*, 253-263.

4. Green, L. S., Oades, L. G., & Grant, A. M. (2006). *Journal of Positive Psychology, 1*(3), 142-149.

5. Grant, A. M., and S. A. O'Connor. "The Differential Effects of Solution-Focused and Problem-Focused Coaching Questions: a Pilot Study with Implications for Practice." *Industrial and Commercial Training*, 42 (2010): 102-111.

6. Peterson, C. & Seligman, M.E.P. (2004) *Character Strengths and Virtues: A handbook and classification.* Washington, DC: American Psychological Association Press and Oxford University Press.

Chapter 2: Move from What's Wrong to What's Strong

1. Seligman, Martin. *Authentic Happiness: Using the New Positive Psychology to Realize Your Potential for Lasting Fulfillment.* New York: Atria Books, 2003; *Flourish: A Visionary New Understanding of Happiness and Well-Being.* New York: Atria Books, 2012.

2. Peterson, C. & Seligman, M.E.P. (2004) *Character Strengths and Virtues: A handbook and classification.* Washington, DC: American Psychological Association Press and Oxford University Press.

3. Seligman, M., Steen, T., Park, N., & Peterson, C. (2005). Positive Psychology Progress: Empirical validation of interventions. American Psychologist, 60, 410-421.

4. VIA Institute on Character. "Character Strengths and Virtues: A Handbook and Classification" Via Character. Accessed on Jun 8, 2015. http://www.viacharacter.org/www/About-Institute/Character-Strengths-and-Virtues.

5. Kauffman, Carol. "Positive Psychology: The Science at the Heart of Coaching." *Evidence Based Coaching Handbook: Putting Best Practices to Work for Your Clients*, edited by D. R. Stober & A. M. Grant 219-253. Hoboken, NJ: John Wiley, 2006.

6. *Too Much of a Good Thing: The Challenge and Opportunity of the Inverted U.* Adam M. Grant and Barry Schwartz *Perspectives on Psychological Science* 2011 6: 61 DOI: 10.1177/1745691 610393523.

7. Biswas-Diener, R., Kashdan, T.B., & Minhas, G. (2011). A dynamic approach to psychological strength development and intervention, The Journal of Positive Psychology, 6 (2), 106-118.

8. P. Zeus and S. Skiffington's (2003) *The Coaching at Work Toolkit*, pp. 285–288); N. M. Tichy's (2002) *The Cycle of Leadership: How Great Leaders Teach Their Companies to Win* (pp. 107–110); and Tichy's (1997) *The Leadership Engine: How Winning Companies Build Leaders at Every Level* (pp. 58–78; 214–218).

9. Clark, M. C. "Off the Beaten Path: Some Creative Approaches to Adult Learning." *New Directions for Adult and Continuing Education* 89 (Spring 2001): 83-91.

10. Dominice, Pierre. Learning from Our Lives: Using Educational Biographies with Adults. San Francisco: Jossey-Bass, 2000.

Chapter 3: The Neuroscience of Optimism

1. Davidson, Richard. "Be Happy Like a Monk." Presentation at Wisconsin Academy, Columbus WI, February 13, 2007.

2. Seligman, M. E. P. *Learned Optimism: How to Change Your Mind and Your Life*. New York: Vintage 1990.

3. Peterson, C. & Seligman, M.E.P. (2004) *Character Strengths and Virtues: A handbook and classification.* Washington, DC: American Psychological Association Press and Oxford University Press; Seligman, M.E.P. (2014). Chris Peterson's unfinished masterwork: The real mental illnesses. The Journal of Positive Psychology. Doi: 10.1080/1743 9760.2014.888582.

4. World Health Organization. "Some Common disorders" The World Health Report. 2001. Accessed Jun 8, 2015. http://www.who.int/whr/2001/chapter2/en/index4.html.

5. Holt-Lunstad, Julianne, Timothy B Smith, and J Bradley Layton. "Social Relationships and Mortality Risk: A meta-analytic Review." *PLoS Medicine* 7, no. 7 (2010). DOI: 10.1371/journal.pmed.1000316.

6. Seligman, Martin. Third World Presentation Congress on Positive Psychology. 2013 International Positive Psychology Association.

7. Williams, R. *Anger Kills: Seventeen Strategies for Controlling the Hostility That Can Harm Your Health.* New York: Harper Torch 1998; Rosenbert, E.L., P. Ekman, et al.(2001), "Linkages between facial expressions of anger and transient myocardial ischemia in men with coronary artery disease," *Emotion* 1:107:15.

8. Wegner, Daniel M., David J. Scheider, Samuel R. Carter, and Teri L. White. "Paradoxical Effects of Thought Suppression." *Journal of Personality and Social Psychology* 53, no. 1, (1987): 5-13.

9. Wenzlaff, Richard M., and Daniel M. Wegner. "Thought Suppression." *Annu. Rev. Psychology* 51 (2000): 59-91.

10. Taylor, Shelley E., and Lien B. Pham. "The Effect of Mental Simulation on Goal-Directed Performance." *Imagination, Cognition and Personality* 18, no. 4 (1999): 253-268.

11. Jenkinson, Caroline E., Andy P. Dickens, Kerry Jones, Jo Thompson-Coon, Rod S. Taylor, Morwenna Rogers, Clare L. Bambra, Iain Lang, and Suzanne H. Richards. "Is Volunteering a Public Health Intervention? A Systematic Review and Meta-Analysis of the Health and Survival of Volunteers." *BMC Public Health* 13, no. 773 (2013): doi:10.1186/1471-2458-13-773.

12. Fredickson, Barbara L. "Flourishing and the Genome" Presentation at Third World Congress on Positive Psychology, Los Angeles, CA 2013.

13. Lawson, Misa. "The Science Behind EBT." Misa Lawson EBT Coach. Accessed Jun 8 2015. http://www.misalawson.com/the-science-behind-ebt/.

14. Ed Diener. Interview. July 9, 2009.

Chapter 4: Coaching the Whole Person

1. CDC "Overweight and Obesity." Centers for Disease Control and Prevention. Last modified Sept 3, 2014. http://www.cdc.gov/ obesity/ data/facts.html.

2. American Heart Association "Smoking: Do You Really Know the Risks?" American Heart Association. Last modified Mar 27, 2015. http://www.heart.org/HEARTORG/GettingHealthy/ QuitSmoking/ QuittingSmoking/Smoking-Do-you-really-know-the-risks_UCM_3 18_Article.jsp.

3. American Diabetes Association "Statistics about Diabetes." American Diabetes Association. Last modified May 18, 2015. http://www. diabetes.org/diabetes-basics/statistics/?loc=db slabnav.

4. Levine, Bruce E. *Surviving America's Depression Epidemic: How to Find Morale, Energy, and Community in a World Gone Crazy*. White River Junction: Chelsea Green Publishing, 2007.

5. "Major Depression Facts: Understanding Clinical (Major) Depression Today." Uncommon Knowledge. Accessed Jun 8, 2015. http:// www.clinical-depression.co.uk/dlp/depression-information/major-depression-facts/.

6. World Health Organization. "Some Common disorders" The World Health Report. 2001. Accessed Jun 8, 2015. http://www.who. int/ whr/2001/chapter2/en/index4.html.

7. Proyer, R. T., F. Gander, S. Wellenzohn, and W. Ruch "What Good Are Character Strengths Beyond Subjective Well-Being? The Contribution of the Good Character on Self-Reported Health Oriented Behavior, Physical Fitness, and the Subjective Health Status." *The Journal of Positive Psychology* 8 (2013): 222-232.

8. Leontopoulou, Sophie and Sofia Triliva. "Explorations of Subjective Well-being and Character Strengths Among a Greek University Student Sample." *International Journal of Well-being* 2, no. 3 (2012): 251-270.

9. Proctor, C., J. Maltby, and P. A. Linley. "Strengths Use as a Predictor of Well-Being and Health-Related Quality of Life." *Journal of Happiness Studies* 10 (2009): 583-630.

10. Hyman, Mark. *The UltraMind Solution. Fix Your Broken Brain by Healing Your Body First*. New York: Scribner 2008.

11. Peterson, C. & Seligman, M.E.P. (2004) *Character Strengths and Virtues: A handbook and classification*. Washington, DC: American Psychological Association Press and Oxford University Press.

12. Steptoe, Andrew, Katie O'Donnell, Ellena Badrick, Meena Kumari, and Michael Marmot. "Neuroendocrine and Inflammatory Factors Associated with Positive Affect in Healthy Men and Women." *American Journal of Epidemiology* 167, no. 1 (2008): 96-102.

13. Cohen, S., Janicki-Deverts, D., Crittenden, C. & Sneed, R. "Personality and Human Immunity." *Oxford Handbook of Psychoneuroimmunology*. New York: Oxford University Press 2012. 146-169.

14. Hyman, Mark. *The UltraMind Solution. Fix Your Broken Brain by Healing Your Body First*. New York: Scribner 2008. 37.

15. Helmrich, Barbara H. "Window of Opportunity? Adolescence, Music and Algebra." *Journal of Adolescent Research* 25, no. 4 (2010): 557-577.

16. Dignity Health "The Healing Power of Kindness" Dignity Health. Accessed Jun 8, 2015. http://www.dignityhealth.org/cm/ content/ pages/healing-power-of-kindness.asp.

17. Ryan, Richard M., Netta Weinstein, Jessy Bernstein, Kirk Warren Brown, Louis Mistretta, and Marylene Gagne. "Vitalizing Effects of Being Outdoors and in Nature." *Journal of Environmental Psychology* 30 (2010): 159-168.

18. Kimsey-House, Henry. Co-Active Coaching: Changing Business, Transforming Lives. Boston: Nicholas Brealy, 2011.

19. Coutu, Diane and Carole Kauffman. "What Can Coaches Do for You?" *Harvard Business Review*, January 2009. https:// hbr.org/2009/01/what-can-coaches-do-for-you.

Part 2

Chapter 5: Authentic Motivation

1. Fry, Maddy. "Bono Biography" @U2. Accessed Jun 8, 2015. http://www.atu2.com/band/bono/.

2. Gilbert, Paul and Liotti Giovanni. "Mentalizing, Motivation, and Social Mentalities: Theoretical Considerations and Implications for Psychotherapy." *Psychology and Psychotherapy: Theory, Research, and Practice* 84 (2011): 9-25.

3. Statistic Brain Research Institute "New Year's Resolution" Statistic Brain Research Institute. Last modified, January 26, 2015. http://www.statisticbrain.com/new-years-resolution-statistics/.

4. Baumeister, Roy F, and John Tierney. *Willpower: Rediscovering the Greatest Human Strength.* London: Penguin Books, 2012.

5. Gallup "Gallup Created the Science of Strengths" Gallup Strengths Center. Accessed Jun 8, 2015. https://www.gallupstrengths center.com/Home/en-US/About/.

6. Mandela, Nelson "Inauguration Speech" Pretoria, South Africa, May 10, 1994.

7. Peterson, C. & Seligman, M.E.P. (2004) *Character Strengths and Virtues: A handbook and classification.* Washington, DC: American Psychological Association Press and Oxford University Press.

8. Mitchell, Edgar. *In the Shadow of the Moon.* Directed by David Sington. New York City, NY: Velocity Thinkfilm, 2008. DVD.

Chapter 6: Comparanoia

1. "Consumer Debt Statistics." Money Zine. Accessed Jun 8, 2015. http://www.money-zine.com/financial-planning/debt consolidation/consumer-debt-statistics/.

2. Board of Governers Federal Reserve System. *Report on the Economic Well-Being of U.S. Households in 2013.* Washington DC: Federal Reserve, 2014.

3. Peterson, Christopher, and Martin Seligman. *Character Strengths and Virtues: A Handbook and Classification.* Washington DC: American Psychological Association, 2004.

Chapter 7: Reframe Failure

1. Zone, Eric. "Without Failure, Jordon Would Be a False Idol." Chicago Tribune May 19, 1997. http://articles.chicago tribune.com/1997-05-19/news/9705190096_1_nike-mere-rumor-driver-s-license.

2. "Thomas Edison" Wikiquote. Last modified May 29 2015. http://en.wikiquote.org/wiki/Thomas_Edison.

3. Covey, Stephen M.R. *The Speed of Trust: The One Thing that Changes Everything.* New York: Free Press 2008.

4. Seligman, Martin. "Building Resilience" *Harvard Business Review*, April 2011. https://hbr.org/2011/04/building-resilience.

5. Peterson, C. & Seligman, M.E.P. (2004) *Character Strengths and Virtues: A handbook and classification.* Washington, DC: American Psychological Association Press and Oxford University Press.

6. Peterson, Christopher, Nansook Park, Nnamdi Pole, Wendy D'Andrea, Martin E. P. Seligman. "Strengths of Character and Posttraumatic Growth." *Journal of Traumatic Stress* 21, no. 2 (2008): 214-217; Tedeschi, R.G. and L. G. Calhoun. *Trauma and Transformation: Growing in the Aftermath of Suffering.* Thousand Oaks CA: Sage 1995.

Chapter 8: Mindful Emotions

1. Niemiec, Ryan M. *Mindfulness and Character Strengths: A Practical Guide to Flourishing. Kirkland: Hogrefe Publishing*, 2013.

2. Young, Shinzen. "Break Through Pain: Practical Steps for Transforming Physical Pain into Spiritual Growth." Shinzen.org. Accessed Jun 8, 2015. http://www.shinzen. org/Articles/artPain.htm.

3. "Sallatha Sutta: The Arrow" (SN 36.6). Translataed from the Pali by Thanissaro Bhikkhu. Access to Insight (Legacy Edition) 30 November 2013.

4. Neff, K. D., and C. K Germer. "Pilot Study and Randomized Controlled Trial of the Mindful Self-Compassion Program." *Journal of Clinical Psychology* 69, no. 1 (2013): 28-44.

5. Neff, K. D. "Development and Validation of a Scale to Measure Self-Compassion." *Self and Identity* 2 (2003): 223-250.

6. Fredrickson, Barbara L., R. A. Mancuso, C. Branigan, and M. M. Tugade. "The Undoing Effect of Positive Emotions." *Motiv Emot.* 24 no. 4 (2000):237-258.

7. Fredrickson, Barbara L., and R. W. Levenson. "Positive Emotions Speed Recovery from the Cardiovascular Sequelae of Negative Emotions." *Cognitive Emotions* 12, no. 2 (1998): 191-220.

8. Peterson, C. & Seligman, M.E.P. (2004) *Character Strengths and Virtues: A handbook and classification.* Washington, DC: American Psychological Association Press and Oxford University Press.

9. Del Monte, Luciano. "Amazing Grace in Mother Teresa" Cross-Training for Life. Accessed Jun. 8 2015. http://coach delmonte. com/2011/03/21/mother-teresas-grace/.

Part 3

Chapter 9: CSQ Fuels EQ

1. Goleman, Daniel. *Emotional Intelligence: Why It Can Matter More than IQ.* New York: Bantam, 2005.

2. Fredrickson, Barbara L. *Positivity: Top-Notch Research Reveals The Upward Spiral that Will Change Your Life.* Edinburgh: Harmony, 2009.

3. Peterson, C. & Seligman, M.E.P. (2004) *Character Strengths and Virtues: A handbook and classification.* Washington, DC: American Psychological Association Press and Oxford University Press.

4. Pope, Alexander. "Thoughts on Various Subjects" *Alexander Pope.* Dublin: Sylvanus Pepyat, 1737.

Chapter: 10 The Smart Swarm

1. *Harvard Business Review* "The Value of Happiness": "How Employee Well-being Drives Profit" Jan-Feb 2012. https://hbr.org/2012/.

2. Killingworth, Matt "The Science Behind a Smile" *Harvard Business Review.* April 2012. https://hbr.org/2012/01/the-science-behind-the-smile.

3. Harzer, C., & Ruch, W. (2013) The application of signature character strengths and positive experiences at work, Journal of Happiness Studies, 14(3), 965-983.

4. Gander, F., Proyer, R. T., Ruch, W., & Wyss, T. (2012). The Good Character at Work: An initial study on the contribution of character strengths in identifying healthy and unhealthy work-related behavior and experience patterns. *International Archives of Occupational and Environmental Health,* 85 (8), 895-904.

5. "Albert Schweitzer-Biographical" Nobel Foundation. Accessed Jun 8, 2015. http://www.nobelprize.org/nobel_prizes/peace/laureates/1952/schweitzer-bio.html.

6. VIA Institute on Character. "Character Strengths and Virtues: A Handbook and Classification" Via Character. Accessed on Jun 8, 2015. http://www.viacharacter.org/www/About-Institute/ Character-Strengths-and-Virtues.

7. Peterson, C. & Seligman, M.E.P. (2004) *Character Strengths and Virtues: A handbook and classification.* Washington, DC: American Psychological Association Press and Oxford University Press.

8. Park, N. and Christopher Peterson. "Character Strengths: Research and Practice." *Journal of College and Character* 10, no. 4 (2009a): n.p.

9. "Tal Ben Shahar." Azquotes. Accessed June 8 2015. http://www.azquotes.com/quote/672859.

10. Cooperrider, D.L. (1990). Positive image, positive action: The affirmative basis of organizing. In S. Srivastva & D. Cooperrider (Eds.), *Appreciative Management and Leadership: The power of positive thought and action in organizations.* John Wiley & Sons.

11. Cooperrider, David. "The Three Circles of Strengths Revolution: Moving from the Micro to the Macro Magnification of Strengths via Appreciative Inquiry." Presentation from VIA Institute on Character. n. d.

Chapter 11: Flow with Strengths

1. Csikszentmihalyi, Mihaly. *Flow: The Psychology of Optimal Experience.* New York: Harper Perennial Modern Classics, 2008.

2. Park, N. and Christopher Peterson. "Character Strengths: Research and Practice." Journal of College and Character 10, no. 4 (2009a): n.p.: Peterson, Christopher, W. Ruch, U. Beerman, N. Park, and M. E. P Seligman. "Strengths of Character, Orientations to Happiness, and Life Satisfaction." Journal of Positive Psychology, 2 (2007): 149-156.

3. Biswas-Diener, R. (2010). Practicing positive psychology coaching: Assessment, activities and strategies for success. Hoboken, New Jersey: John Wiley and Sons.

4. Ed Diener. Interview. July 9, 2009.

5. Benson, Herbert and Miriam Z. Klipper. *The Relaxation Response.* New York: HarperTorch, 2000.

6. Davidson, Richard. "Be Happy Like a Monk." Presentation at Wisconsin Academy, Columbus WI, February 13, 2007.

7. Peterson, C. & Seligman, M.E.P. (2004) *Character Strengths and Virtues: A handbook and classification.* Washington, DC: American Psychological Association Press and Oxford University Press.

8. Lehrer, Jonah. "The Eureka Hunt." *The New Yorker.* July 28, 2008. http://www.newyorker.com/magazine/2008/07/28/the-eureka-hunt.

9. Wrzesniewski, A., McCaluley, C., Rozin, P., & Schwartz, B. (1997). Jobs, Careers, and Callings: People's relations to their work. Journal of research in personality, 31 (1), 21-33.

10. Diener, Ed. *Happiness—Unlocking the Mysteries of Psychological Wealth.* Hoboken, NJ: Wiley Blackwell, 2008.

11. "About Us." Virgin. Accessed Jun 9, 2015. https://www.virgin.com/about-us.

Chapter 12: Ride the Wave to Uncommon Performance

1. Bracken, Sam. *My Orange Duffel Bag: A Journey to Radical Change.* New York: Crown Archetype 2012.

2. Olivero, Gerald, K Denise Bane, and Richard E Kopelman *Public Personnel Management*; Washington: Winter 1997.

3. "VIA Classification of Character Strengths, Strengths Building" VIA Institute of Character. Accessed June 5, 2015. http://www.viacharacter.org/www/Character-Strengths/VIA-Classification#nav.

4. Coutu, Diane and Carole Kauffman. "What Can Coaches Do for You?" *Harvard Business Review*, January 2009. https://hbr.org/2009/01/what-can-coaches-do-for-you.

5. Peterson, C. & Seligman, M.E.P. (2004) *Character Strengths and Virtues: A handbook and classification.* Washington, DC: American Psychological Association Press and Oxford University Press.

6. Seligman, M., Steen, T., Park, N., & Peterson, C. (2005). Positive Psychology Progress: Empirical validation of interventions. American Psychologist, 60, 410-421.

7. Gander, Fabian, Rene T. Proyer, Willibald Ruch, and Tobias Wyss. "Strength-Based Positive Interventions: Further Evidence for Their Potential in Enhancing Well-Being and Alleviated Depression." Springer Science Business Media B.V. 2012. DOI 10.1007/s10902-012-9380-0.

About Authentic Strengths Advantage®

Our mission is helping people explore, empower and engage their character strengths personally and professionally to create positive, measurable and sustainable results.

We deliver transformational, evidence-based coaching, training and tools that leverage character strengths in order to maximize human contributions and fulfillment—at work and in life.

The Authentic Strengths Advantage® is a game changer because appreciating and leveraging strengths creates a culture of mutual respect where people are empowered to make their distinct contributions. Our process and tools inspire people to bring their authentic best selves to work and life, creating the conditions for sustainable high performance—the key to human motivation and engagement.

Visit us at authenticstrengths.com to learn more. Join our learning community to share your insights and successes using the Authentic Strengths Advantage® tools in this book.

About VIA

In 1998, Dr. Neal H. Mayerson and then President of the American Psychological Association, Dr. Martin E.P. Seligman conceived the establishment of a robust effort to explore what is best about human beings and how we can use those best characteristics to build our best lives. They launched an effort of unprecedented magnitude to lay the groundwork for the new science of positive psychology. Dr. Mayerson created a nonprofit organization (now the VIA Institute on Character) to do this work and provided the funding to support Dr. Seligman in orchestrating a diverse collection of scholars and practitioners who took three years and more than a million dollars to complete the development of the VIA Classification of Character Strengths and Virtues and the VIA Surveys for adults and youth. The enormous response of people worldwide taking the survey has made it clear that VIA's work is resonating broadly and deeply.

The mission of the VIA Institute on Character is to advance both the science and the practice of character strengths to help people construct lives that are fulfilling. The nonprofit offers the scientifically validated VIA Survey, free of charge, across the globe. Millions of people from more than 200 countries have taken the survey, now translated into many languages.

ABOUT THE AUTHOR

Fatima Doman, Founder and CEO of Authentic Strengths Advantage®, shares insights from her two decades of experience working with Fortune 100 and 500 companies as an Executive Coach. She has served as Director of Certification for the internationally acclaimed 7 Habits of Highly Effective People Training Program and Co-founder of the FranklinCovey Global Executive Coaching Practice. Fatima's coaching specialty areas include: leveraging client strengths through positive psychology coaching, emotional intelligence, whole life vitality, energy management, appreciative inquiry and positive leadership.

Fatima believes that self-awareness plays a key role in becoming an exceptional coach, and that each of us can develop our strengths to realize our aspirations and address our challenges. Drawing on groundbreaking positive psychology and neuroscience research, Fatima reveals pathways to improving human performance and relationships. She demonstrates how engaging your strengths while appreciating strengths in others boosts your emotional intelligence and dramatically transforms your effectiveness at work and in life. She now spends much of her time conducting strengths coaching and positive leadership training with executives around the world. Fatima's greatest fulfillment comes from enjoying time with her husband and two sons.